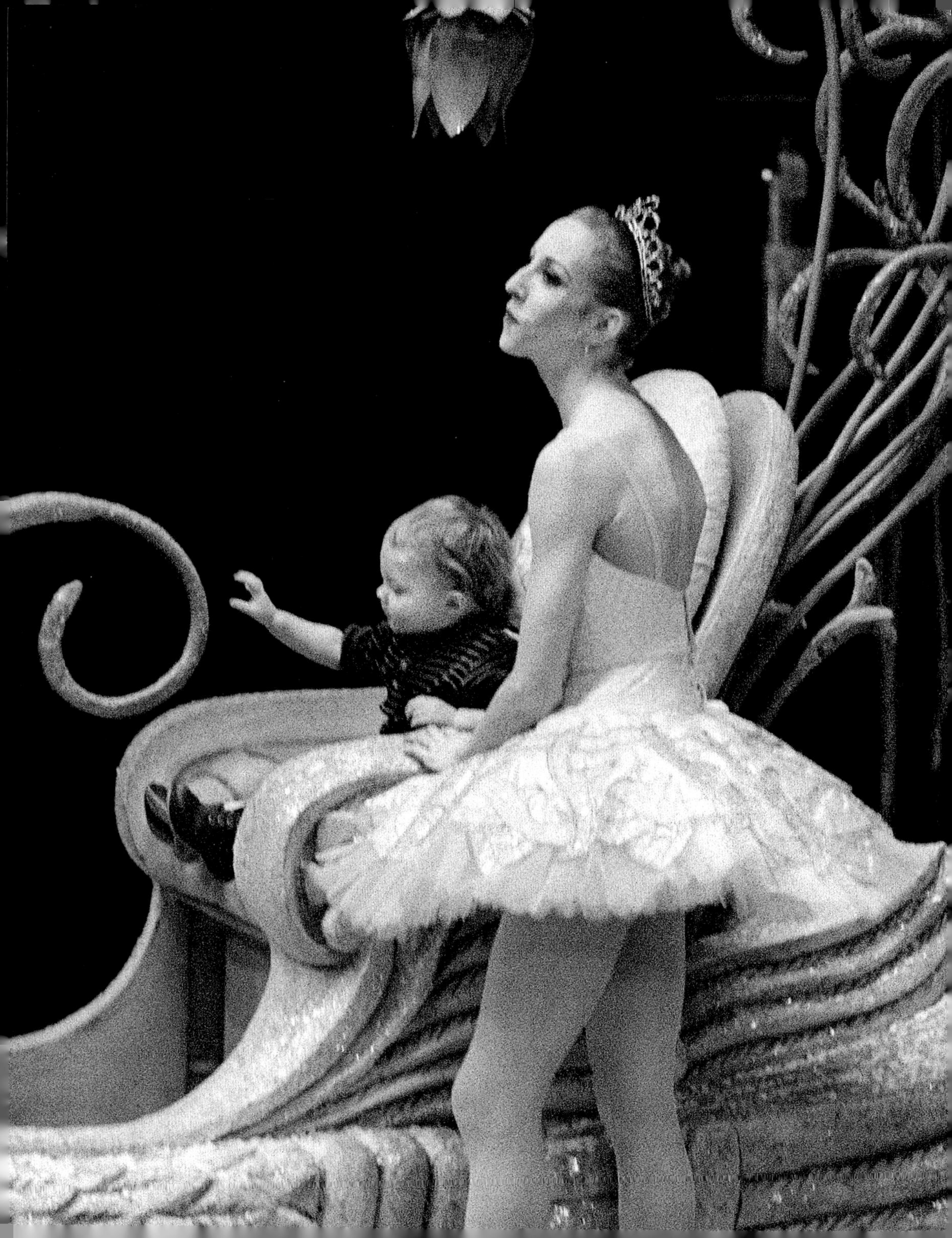

BALANCING ACTS

Three Prima Ballerinas Becoming Mothers

LUCY GRAY

Foreword by Hilton Als

PRINCETON ARCHITECTURAL PRESS · NEW YORK

FOR THE CHILDREN:

Kate, Mathew, Rachel, Nicholas, and Zachary

Published by
Princeton Architectural Press
37 East Seventh Street
New York, New York 10003

Visit our website at www.papress.com.

Printed and bound in China by
1010 Printing International Limited
18 17 16 15 4 3 2 1 First edition

Editor: Sara Stemen
Designer: Mia Johnson

Special thanks to: Meredith Baber, Sara Bader, Nicola Bednarek Brower, Janet Behning, Megan Carey, Carina Cha, Andrea Chlad, Tom Cho, Barbara Darko, Benjamin English, Russell Fernandez, Will Foster, Jan Cigliano Hartman, Jan Haux, Diane Levinson, Jennifer Lippert, Katharine Myers, Jaime Nelson, Rob Shaeffer, Marielle Suba, Kaymar Thomas, Paul Wagner, Joseph Weston, and Janet Wong of Princeton Architectural Press —Kevin C. Lippert, publisher

Library of Congress Cataloging-in-Publication Data
Gray, Lucy, 1955-
Balancing acts / Lucy Gray.
pages cm
ISBN 978-1-61689-254-8 (alk. paper)
1. Ballet—Social aspects. 2. Ballerinas—Social conditions. 3. Ballerinas—California—San Francisco. 4. San Francisco Ballet. 5. Women—Social conditions. 6. Working mothers—United States. 7. Motherhood. I. Title.
GV1787.G687 2015
792.8—dc23
2014017081

CONTENTS

FOREWORD

HILTON ALS

I think it was the late poet and publisher Patrick O'Connor who was the first person to take me to see live ballet; I was still in my teens, but he wasn't the first person in my life to love dance—my mother was, but she didn't have access to tickets, she wouldn't have known how to get to Lincoln Center unaided, but we had a television set, and that was our portal into the world of culture our mother adored; she had six children, and there was no money, but among the vital things she taught us in our relatively limited world was that poverty didn't mean shit when it came to the imagination, poverty can't kill your dreams, or curtail anything; art making was a way to transcend the world's strictures, and how exciting was it that there was an art—the dance—that celebrated the body in space and the body's ability to change the atmosphere; and I remember now, as I try to write this sentence that is an attempt to linguistically approximate the joy one finds in Lucy Gray's evocative photographs of women as mothers, as dancers, as performers, as choreographers, as muses—sometimes all at once, because that's what these women look like, one beautiful sentence unwinding in an atmosphere of work and play and realized enjoyment—the enjoyment one feels doing what one means to do—a sentence that's tied to the rise and fall of the breath, which these dancers understand, too; it's their breathing that informs the dance—I can hear their breath in these pictures (can't you?); in any case, in those old but not forgotten days of my mother and the television and her dreams, I remember hearing, from another relative, that my mother had wanted to be a dancer when she was a girl—she loved social dancing more than anything, they called her the girl of a hundred steps, and in my imagination I see her unwinding like a ribbon at the Savoy Ballroom in Harlem (this would have been in the 1940s and right after the war); she was a girl then, wearing saddle shoes and bobby sox, and maybe she had on a little black skirt, too—she liked black—and maybe she had a ribbon in her hair, the way certain of the prima ballerinas in Lucy Gray's book wear ribbons, but unlike the dancers who mother in Gray's pictures, my mother had to be her own prima ballerina; there was no choreographer who contributed to the dance of her life, but dance she did; years passed, and I met a gay man named Patrick O'Connor who loved glamour and movement; he took me to the New York City Ballet and appeared to be so interested in what I had to say about the performance that it was as if someone had turned an enormous spotlight on me—his attention exposed my brain to itself, like a flower looking at itself, and what we watched in those New York City Ballet afternoons and evenings were ballerinas like Darci Kistler and Lourdes Lopez and—who else? well, it was a world only Joseph Cornell could have imagined, all that fairy dust and the sound of wooden pointe on the floor, the perspiration dancers wear like a second coat of makeup; and it was through Patrick that I met the great dance critic Edwin Denby, who was thin and beautiful and white-haired—Patrick had published his books in paperback—and when I wrote him a fan letter to thank him for his work, asking Could I see him? Edwin Denby told Patrick that as much as he loved the young, and my note, he was too old to make new friends, but there was his work, and in those marvelous pieces, there were descriptions of the prima ballerina, and how important it was to look at her line and openness of expression, and one sees what Denby described in his books in Lucy Gray's photographs, an openness of expression that's italicized by the openness of expression one sees in the dancers' children, their sweet desire to emulate their mothers in their toddler-sized awkwardness—what a dream for a boy or a little girl, to have access to this world of make-believe, just as I had access to my mother's make-believe as she watched Margot Fonteyn or whomever on television dancing, dancing, dancing, as if there were no such thing as unhappiness in this world, dancing as though there were no tomorrow, but the dancers in Lucy Gray's images know there's a tomorrow: it's standing, sometimes, right in front of them, baby legs stretching to meet a mother's legs, legs that can perform feats their baby legs can't (and isn't that a mother, the woman who can perform feats your baby legs can never catch up to?); one of the great things about Lucy Gray's images are that they are free of competition—all of the dancers captured are supporting their colleagues' right to movement, since their freedom informs their own—but they are not free of joy, which is essential if you want to mother, if you want to dance, if you want to become anything; joy is what carries you through the hard work of living, the hard work that must go into the imagination to make the dream real; in 1944 Marianne Moore, writing of the legendary Anna Pavlova and the "exacting discipline" of dance, said: "[Pavlova] was compelling because of spiritual force that did not need to be mystery, she so affectionately informed her technique with poetry"; and isn't that the point of anything: to inform it with poetry, whether that poetry be a mother's dreams for her children, or a stagestruck gay man's dreams for his adopted child, or the poetry one sees in Lucy Gray's subjects' grown-up or baby faces?

INTRODUCTION

When I first started this project, I was a working mother, like the ballerinas in this book, although my boys were a few years older than their newborns. From the start we had a natural affinity and, yes, we did talk about our children, but I was not inspired by our likenesses. It was our differences that made me want to photograph these women and keep at it for fourteen years. It was my hope, even my intention, that they would reframe my views, open my mind, and help me let go of prejudice. They did not disappoint.

As a proud feminist, I once held negative, unfounded beliefs about ballerinas. I viewed them as self-centered and self-destructive—chain smokers who drove themselves to maintain the skinny bodies of little girls. Their single-minded devotion to their craft seemed akin to an addiction, and I was disturbed by their apparent willingness to starve themselves for the approval of male directors, as part of a culture that glorified sacrifice as essential to the artistic process.

Then in the fall of 1999, while shopping at a local market, I met Katita Waldo, a prima ballerina for the San Francisco Ballet. I couldn't miss noticing her: she was thin and pale—she looked destitute—and was carrying her infant. But as I got closer, her skin seemed to glow under her halo of red hair. I was with my three-year-old son and his friend, who introduced us: the child and the dancer were neighbors.

Katita intrigued me, and I wanted to photograph her with her son, James. I ignored everything I thought I knew about ballerinas and opened myself to discovering the reality of her life. I asked her to participate in a long-term photographic and interviewing process that would focus on her as both a dancer and a mother: how motherhood had impacted her creative expression, her body, and her perspective. She told me there were two other dancers at the San Francisco Ballet who'd recently had children, Tina LeBlanc and Kristin Long—all three were enthusiastic to be a part of this project and offered me extraordinary creative freedom to chronicle this chapter of their lives.

• • •

A ballerina's belief in her power is reflected in her body. She spends her life—often from the age of three or four—navigating the world physically. Letting go and gaining weight and then pushing another being out of her is anathema to every experience she's ever had. Further, her physical desirability is essential to being cast by her company's artistic director—almost invariably a *he* in this country—who has the latitude to be as unpredictable and capricious as he wishes. A ballerina's hours are inflexible and long, and her pay fluctuates. She experiences enormous pressure to perform flawlessly onstage. This affects the roles she's given and her salary. Not only does having a baby increase the possibility of injuries, it raises a host of anxieties—that while she is on leave she might be altogether forgotten and replaced.

Then if she decides to overcome all of these worries, there is the challenge of getting pregnant in a window of a month or two, so she can keep dancing through, say, her second month; have the baby in the summer (while the company is on leave between performance seasons); and be back onstage dancing the following winter. Only then might she continue to get paid through the process. In spite of all of these tangible professional risks, each of these women had—at what appeared to be the height of her success in a ballet company that was working to become world-class—decided to have a baby. Their careers represent one of the toughest possible situations for a working mother. If these women could balance work and parenthood—and succeed at both—then surely many of us, among the tens of millions of working mothers in this country, can do so, too.

What none of us involved in this project could have anticipated is that all three ballerinas improved as dancers *after* they had children. Local newspaper critics wrote rave reviews: "Tina LeBlanc [is] dancing like gangbusters since her return from maternity leave." Her dancing that year was described as "poetic"; Kristin Long's as "brilliant"; and Katita Waldo's as a "marvel." They all felt that the break from dancing—the first since they were toddlers—was rejuvenating in the extreme, and each dancer found that the new commitments in her personal life freed her onstage. They were no longer dancing just for themselves. Dancing was put in perspective; as Tina described it, "I wasn't saving a life. I was entertaining people. I could see that after I had my son, Marinko." Work provided time away from home, which made returning to being a mother fun, too. Responsibilities at the SFB and at home were enlivened and enriched by each other.

Even so, regrouping muscles, redeveloping stamina on toes, and living primarily on a water diet again were hard-won gains. Helgi Tomasson, the artistic director and principal choreographer of the SFB, helped each of the dancers financially work out how they could continue at the company. They were grateful for his understanding, which they attributed, at least in part, to his own dedication as a parent. The ballerinas and I hoped their decision would make a lasting impression on the company, affecting dancers long after their own children had grown. But since Katita, Tina, and Kristin became mothers, it has once again become noteworthy for principal dancers at SFB, as well as in other leading American dance companies (with the exceptions of New York City Ballet under the artistic direction of Peter Martins and Houston Ballet, whose Australian director, Stanton Welch, is the son of dancers), to decide to have babies. Although Tomasson hasn't directly discouraged ballerinas from becoming mothers, I have heard from ballerinas, off the record, that they are afraid to do so.

Their fears are supported historically, although they are unique to American ballet. (In Europe, a prima ballerina's decision to become a mother is a frequent occurrence, a reality woven into the fabric of company life.) The complication in this country, ironically, stems from the galvanizing force of George Balanchine, a Russian immigrant and an extraordinarily prolific choreographer.

He was the creator of the New York City Ballet, where, with the help of a grant from the Ford Foundation in the 1970s, he educated audiences, dancers, and artistic directors about ballet. He had been trained as a dancer in imperial St. Petersburg but after the revolution, as Jennifer Homans describes in *Apollo's Angels: A History of Ballet*, "Balanchine's bold choreographic innovations" were "disapproved of" and he "took the first opportunity out." It was Balanchine, who expected an ethereal, almost spiritual, quality from his dancers—on and off the stage. Homans writes, "He was not interested in ordinary people or real social situations.... For him, ballet was an art of angels, of idealized and elevated human figures, beautiful, chivalric, and above all, strictly formal."

This pursuit of perfection was, no doubt, part of his allure for the dancers. The punishing physical labor he exacted, the demand to be unnaturally thin, and the incredible skills he required—an extreme turnout of the feet is just one example—were sacrifices a ballerina might even take pride in if she could feel gossamer wings onstage. To hold to this standard, Balanchine told ballerinas in his company that a serious relationship with a man would ruin a dancer's career, that a bond outside ballet would steal her focus. However, he slept with countless dancers in his employ and married four. One of his favorites, Suzanne Farrell, married another dancer. She was then "effectively dismissed," wrote Jennifer Dunning in the *New York Times*. Six years later she returned alone. Allegra Kent, the only woman principal in his company who chose to have three children, reported in her autobiography, *Once a Dancer*, that when she returned to work after having her second, in 1964, Balanchine told her, "Now, Allegra, no more babies. Enough is enough. Babies are for Puerto Ricans."

Devotees of Balanchine believe that ballet has never been as fine an art form before or since his time in New York. He not only left a mystique and a legacy, but he choreographed more than four hundred dances, many of which are still performed today. Balanchine directed Tomasson for fifteen years before he retired as a dancer in 1985 and took over at San Francisco Ballet, where, with the help of Tina, Kristin, Katita, and other dancers, he elevated the company to one of the world's greatest producers of classical ballet, alongside New York City Ballet and American Ballet Theatre. As is true of the artistic director of any ballet company, Tomasson is the sole arbiter of taste. He may decide to keep a dancer, or not, and has various ways to let her go if he chooses. There are some safeguards for a dancer with seniority, but these protections, at best, may keep her employed an extra year. At the beginning of the season, she will know, with reasonable assurance, the parts in which she will be cast. If he doesn't want a dancer in the company, even if she has seniority, he can stop giving her roles. This can be humiliating—often the reason for a dancer to leave a company. The American Guild of Musical Artists (the dancers' union) holds no power over directors' decisions.

This is why it was so brave that Katita, Tina, and Kristin took the risk to pursue what *they* wanted—and so striking that Tomasson responded with kindness and ingenuity. They each recounted his reaction when they shared their plans to become mothers: "Is this really what you want?" he asked. When they answered, "Yes," he helped make it possible. He offered Kristin the role of principal dancer, thereby increasing her salary. He cast Tina in roles that allowed her to continue to dance while pregnant (as well as after she gave birth to Marinko), and colleagues in the office babysat until she found a nanny. Katita was also offered help with her schedule to maximize her pay. Tomasson and the ballerinas' husbands provided the essential support the women needed to make their decision to become mothers a viable professional reality. The father of Tina's sons, Marco Jerkunica; Katita's partner, Marshall Crutcher; and Kristin's first husband, Michael Locicero, all took on the heavy day-to-day parenting and loved it, which gave Tomasson the gift of continuing to work with his prized dancers. And the children had the good fortune to grow up with this extraordinary dimension of theater enriching their lives.

• • •

In planning this project, it was important to me to document the full span of the prima ballerinas' fierce creativity—from performing onstage to giving birth, and back again. Since 1999 I have turned my lens on them, bearing witness to some of the most dramatic moments in their lives, as well as the quieter, meditative ones: Katita wrestles with stage fright. We see Tina, as the mother of a toddler, being taught a dance by her idol, choreographer Natalia Makarova—the famous Russian ballerina who came to America in 1970; had a child in 1978, when she was thirty-seven; didn't retire from dancing until she was fifty; wrote an autobiography; created a BBC television series; and narrated award-winning audiobooks for children. Kristin gets a divorce and marries again, this time to the freshly hired, very popular conductor at the ballet, Martin West, and they have two more children. I watched these women develop as mothers and dancers; just as movingly, I observed their children as they grew from tiny newborns to towering teenagers with their own professional dreams starting to develop. Each of the dancers eventually retired, and I was there when the ballet slipper came off for the last time. All three teach ballet now: Katita helps performers learn the dances at SFB as a ballet mistress; Tina teaches at San Francisco Ballet's school; and Kristin teaches at City Ballet School in San Francisco.

I chose the photographs I thought would express a sense of drama and reflect the human story. The words *theater*, *stage*, and *performance* are common to both hospitals and ballet; each one is an arena where spectacular, life-changing events occur. Once you have watched these dancers onstage, observing them *perform* in the hospital makes an extraordinary contrast. The breadth of these women's experiences is vast and unique. Look at how much one person can create! And when Kristin does a tour jeté over her son in a rehearsal room, the thrill in her dual achievements transcends that particular space and creates a frisson that working parents all over the world can recognize.

THE DANCERS

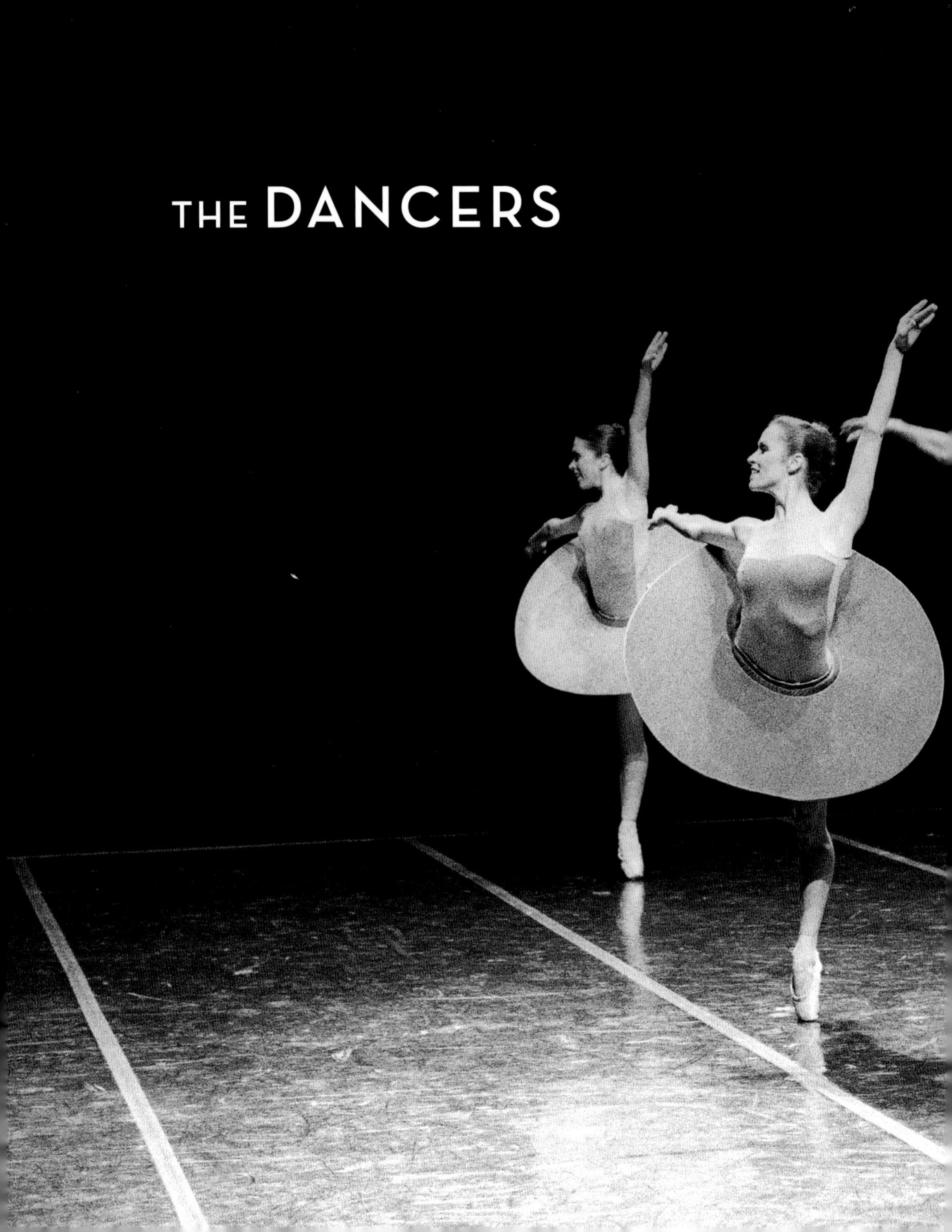

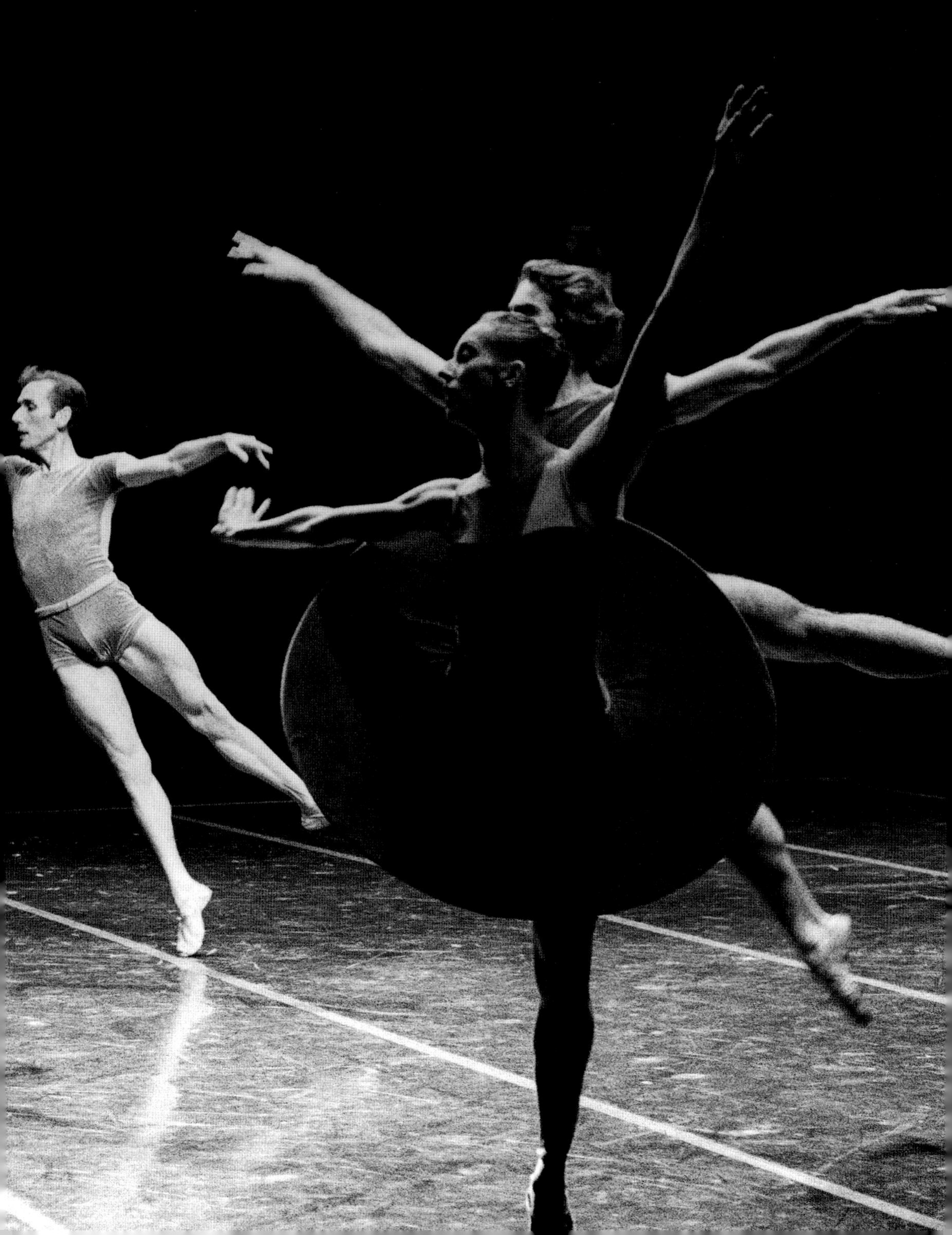

For their work in William Forsythe's *The Vertiginous Thrill of Exactitude*, Tina LeBlanc, Kristin Long, and Katita Waldo, with colleagues Gennadi Nedvigin and Roman Rykine, received the 2002 Outstanding Achievement in Performance—Ensemble award, given by San Francisco's Isadora Duncan Dance Awards Committee.

"We have a little joke in the company about this dance. We say only a mother can do Vertiginous *because, having given birth, she's the one who'll know how to breathe through these lightning-fast routines."*

—FROM TINA'S ACCEPTANCE SPEECH

Previous pages, front row, from left: Kristin Long, Tina LeBlanc, and Katita Waldo; back row: Parrish Maynard and Gonzalo Garcia, in a dress rehearsal of *The Vertiginous Thrill of Exactitude* (William Forsythe) at the War Memorial Opera House in San Francisco. (2001)

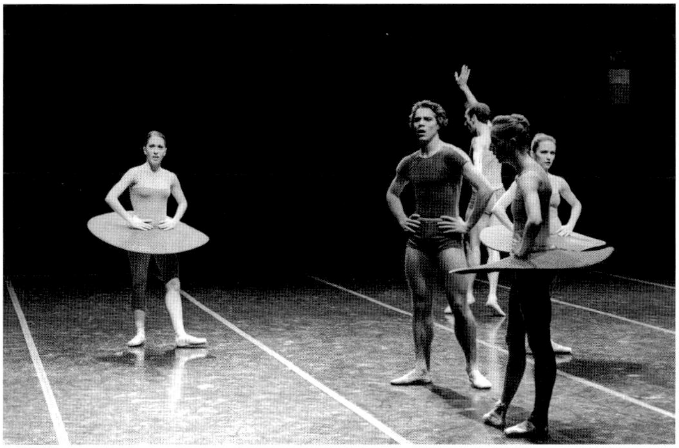

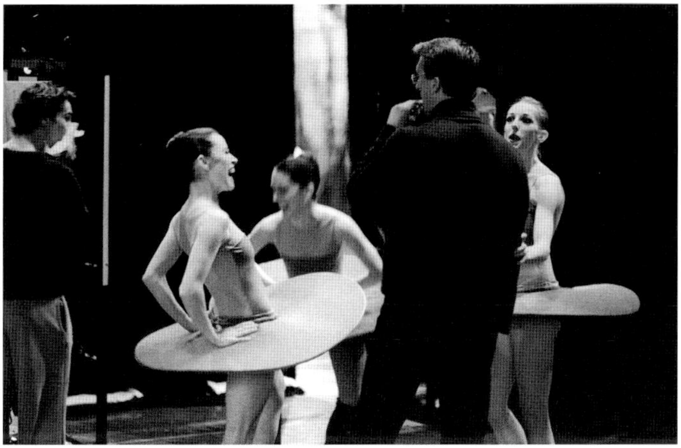

From left: Kristin, Gonzalo, Parrish, Katita, and Tina in *The Vertiginous Thrill of Exactitude*. After the curtain comes down, the dancers catch their breaths.

Moments later: Gonzalo, Tina, Kristin, and Katita. Ballet master Ashley Wheater (with his back turned), who has recently retired as a dancer at San Francisco Ballet, knows how to give notes that make the dancers laugh. He would later become the artistic director of the Joffrey Ballet. (2001)

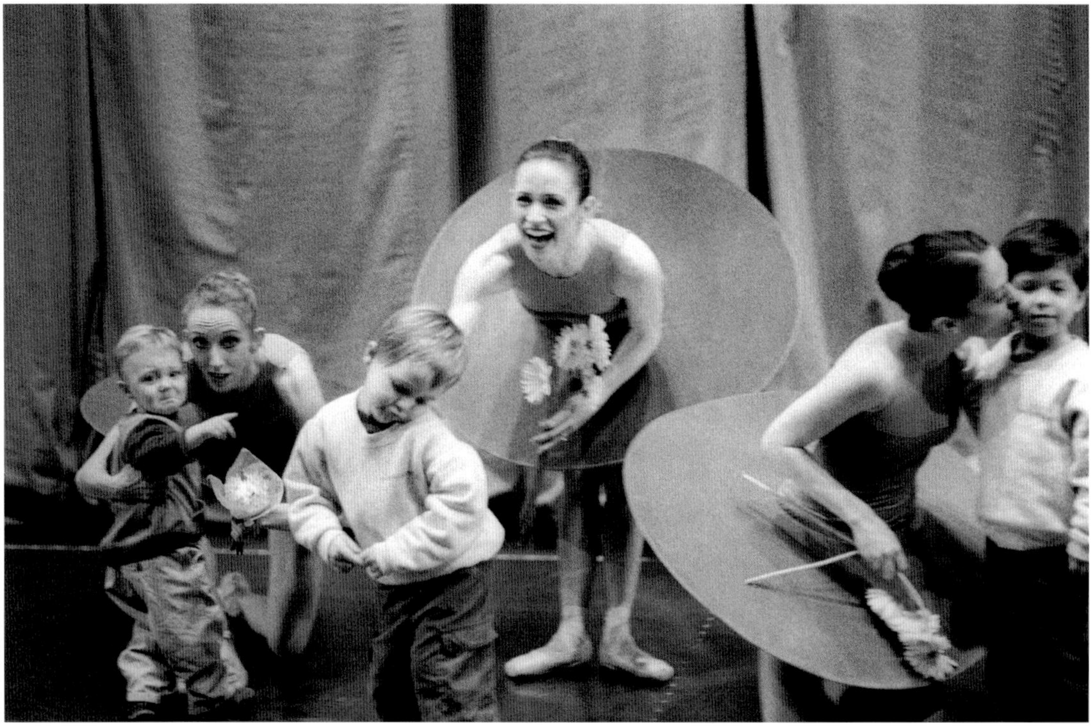

All have sons: Katita Waldo and James Crutcher; Tina LeBlanc and Marinko Jerkunica; Kristin and Kai Long, backstage after a performance of *The Vertiginous Thrill of Exactitude*. (2002)

"For anyone who is thinking about having a baby while you're still dancing, we're here to show you that it can be done."

—FROM KRISTIN'S ACCEPTANCE SPEECH

KRISTIN LONG

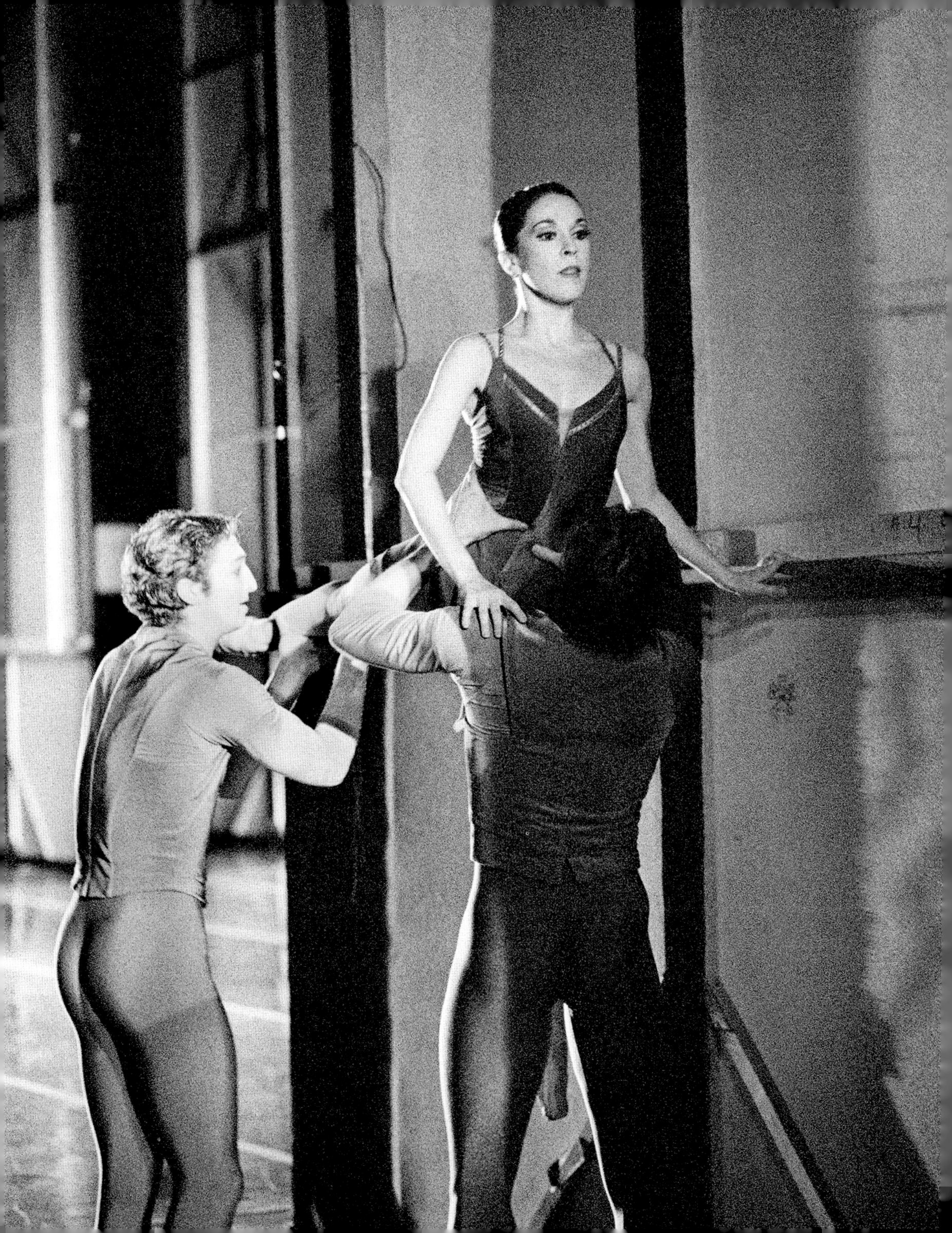

JUL 31, 1972	Born in Altoona, Pennsylvania
1979	Starts at Allegheny Ballet Academy in Altoona under Artistic Director Deborah Anthony
1986	Studies at Central Pennsylvania Youth Ballet in Carlisle, Pennsylvania, under Artistic Director Marcia Dale Weary
1987	Accepted at San Francisco Ballet; studies with Larissa Skalenskaya, Irina Jacobson
1989	Named apprentice at SFB under Artistic Director Helgi Tomasson
1990	Joins SFB; receives Princess Grace Foundation Award
1992	Promoted to soloist at SFB under Artistic Director Helgi Tomasson
1995	Meets Michael Locicero
1996	Marries Michael Locicero
AUG 27, 1997	Gives birth to Kai Seamus Long
1999	Made Principal at SFB under Artistic Director Helgi Tomasson
2001-02 SEASON	Receives Isadora Duncan Dance Award
2002	Meets Martin West professionally while a guest dancer at the English National Ballet
2005	Martin West becomes Music Director and Principal Conductor at SFB; Kristin separates from Michael Locicero
2006	Begins dating Martin West
2008	Divorces Michael Locicero
SEP 23, 2009	Gives birth to Hannah Elizabeth Long West
FEB 22, 2011	Gives birth to Jonah Sebastian Long West
2012	Retires and becomes Level V Instructor at City Ballet School—San Francisco under Artistic Director Galina Alexandrova
2013	Marries Martin West

KRISTIN LONG | APRIL 2002

When I was really little I danced around like a nut. I was probably a lot like Kai in that way. We used to go to country-western concerts. We'd sit in the front row, and I would never be in my seat. I'd be standing up and totally getting down.

My mom was a housewife. My dad worked for the family bus company. I wonder how I got this far in the arts, because they had nothing to do with the arts. We didn't even listen to music that much. We listened to music like every other family, but it wasn't a big part of our lives.

My mom and dad enrolled my older sister and me in gymnastics. My dad was very athletic; I'm sure he wanted us to do something athletic. They decided to enroll us in ballet, just to check it out. So I did gymnastics and ballet, and went back and forth. After a year, that was it: no more gymnastics. I wanted to do only ballet. I was eight. It was weird that there was a good ballet school in Altoona, Pennsylvania. I probably became the first dancer who ever made it from that school, professionally. I was just obsessed.

My older sister quit ballet about a year after she started. She just didn't like it; she essentially became your normal teenager. I was never your normal teenager. I went to ballet immediately after school, and I was there from 4:00 to 9:00 p.m.

By thirteen I would go away every summer to study. The School of American Ballet was very hard to get into; I got in one summer and I hated it. It was all about how you looked rather than how you danced. Down to "Your head's too big for your body." It didn't make you feel like you wanted to dance. It was all about if you were skinny enough, if you had arched feet, the whole thing. If

I'd grown up in New York, where they were concentrating on your head size, I might have quit. I was never your beanpole little girl. Growing up in a small town and not knowing how scrutinized you could be in this profession pushed me to keep doing it, to keep loving it.

I came out here to San Francisco when I was fifteen to study with the San Francisco Ballet. I had a great time, and I loved it, and then I got a full scholarship for the year. My parents knew from my ballet teacher that if I was going to pursue ballet, I needed to do these sorts of things.

It happened perfectly. I couldn't ask for anything more, because I got here, and Helgi [Tomasson] really, really liked me, right away. He saw me in our student demo, which happened in May, then I started working with the company. A dancer got injured before they were going on a tour to the Kennedy Center, and so they took me. Then they were going to Hawaii, and someone else got injured, and I essentially did a soloist part. Helgi had faith in me. He liked the fact that I was gutsy and I seemed so natural.

When I was about twenty I went through a really hard time because I suddenly realized: Oh, my God—this is all I've ever done all my life, and I don't have another life. When I was going through that period, it was bizarre to me that the only place I really felt comfortable with myself was onstage. Outside of that I didn't know who the hell I was. I didn't have Kristin without the ballet. That was really scary. It was a horrible time for me.

By the time I was twenty-three, I thought, You know what? I don't love to dance. I was dancing only to be thin. I'd go to aerobics class before ballet, at six o'clock in the morning. So I took a leave of absence. I said to Helgi, "I don't want to dance. I'm not happy dancing. I need to be happy. I need to figure this out." That's when I got to know that Kristin could be someone other than a ballet dancer. I didn't need to be so overly obsessed with dancing, because it brought me down. Balance was good. And then it was thrown in my face when I had Kai, because I had to have balance. Had I not had Kai, I might still be obsessive.

I'd just come back from my leave of absence in 1995 when I broke my foot. I was living in San Francisco, and Michael was living in New York. We were engaged. I went to New York for the holidays. A month later: pregnant. Total surprise. I thought, "This is not the greatest timing to have a baby," but I still wasn't sure I wanted to continue with my career. I was struggling, sort of burnt out. So we decided to have the baby.

There was a part of me that wanted to stay in New York, where Michael was selling stocks on Wall Street. I'd take care of the baby, we'd stay there for two years, and I'd slowly get back in shape and figure out what I wanted to do, dancewise. I really wasn't sure I wanted to come back to San Francisco. That was the plan until a month before I had the baby, when Michael said, "I am so unhappy. I can't work on Wall Street. I'll be a terrible father." It was wearing him out physically. At that point I hadn't danced for half a year, so I was really ready to go back, and I said, "Yeah, let's give it a shot." I had missed it a lot.

Three weeks after I gave birth, I started taking class. I had the mornings with Kai, then I would drop him with a different person every day—Michael's friends and mine. My little sister also was living in New York. It was getting to be winter, and there Kai was in his little snowsuit on the subway. I could drop him anywhere, and he was fine. He was the easiest kid.

I loved the teacher. He had his own little modern company in New York but taught a ballet class. It was all modern dancers. Not one single classical ballet dancer—so healthy for me. All Mark Morris type of dancers. Totally cool, accepting of their bodies, and here I was trying to get back into shape. The body-issue thing was hard for me, but I never felt pressured. The weight came off easily. I don't think I would have had the confidence that I have if I'd been here doing it, in my environment around all the ballet dancers. I needed to be away.

We came back to San Francisco when Kai was four months old. I felt things would be different because I had Kai. It inspired me. I think with anything in life, if you're really excited about it or really driven, it comes. I would advise everyone to take a leave of absence, although every director would kill me. I would say, "Go for it, take a year." Dancers freak if they're out for four months; they think they'll never be able to dance the same again, but I'm dancing better than I ever have. And I think it's because I took that break. I took yoga, I read a lot, I hung out in New York. I needed to do that. Then I had the baby, and Kai is amazing. He added so much to my life.

I was surprised how easy it was to get back. I wasn't working six-hour days like I am now. It was a nice schedule. I'd work for a few hours, and then I'd come home and be with my baby. I'd get to see him, I'd get to hang out. What could be better?

A lot of that had to do with Michael being so incredible. He had the time to be with Kai, and he loved it. So I had the freedom to do what I needed to—and the biggest thing: I never had to worry when he was sick. Michael worried more for everyone. I never felt that way. And Michael brought Kai to see me dance, which made me happier than anything in the world. Just knowing they were out there.

I find it harder to be a mom now that Kai is five. When he was six months old, I could be rolling and stretching on the floor and still doing something with him. Now I have to go home and play basketball, play soccer. I work hard to find activities with him that aren't physical. I don't want to go home and say, "Mommy's too tired," but I played baseball with him one weekend, and I totally wrecked my arm. I was swinging so hard. Every muscle in my body hurts from dance, and I can't afford to get injured. So I am really creative. He'll cook with me now. We do art projects, and we read, and I'll throw the baseball to him.

Kai has gotten so much from watching me dance, seeing me do something that I love to do, which I think is so important. Also, hearing classical music all the time, being around the orchestra, he's developed relationships with all the orchestra members. And he dances around like a nut. He definitely has it in his blood. He's literally putting his ballet shoes on after dinner, but when I ask, "Do you want to take ballet class?" he says, "No." I say, "So why do you dance so much?" "Because I love it."

KRISTIN LONG | AUGUST 2013

I always felt free on the stage. Hannah makes me watch—"Mommy, *Swan Lake*! I want to see again!" So we sit and watch it, and when I watch it, I really miss that feeling—despite the nerves beforehand—of just getting there, that moment of being onstage and feeling the audience with you. Portraying a role and getting really involved in that.

I was always about expression. If there's anything that came most naturally to me, it was that. Maybe through the later years that shifted, which was a sad thing for me, because I lost sight of that a little bit. And I was technically fine, too. I never had the perfect body.

It wasn't until after I had Kai that [Helgi] suddenly said, "You look different, you look better." I had cheekbones, and what had been breasts that were higher up dropped down, which is, of course, what they want a ballerina to look like. I guess that had stopped me, in his mind, from making me a soloist or principal. Because I had done so much soloist work and principal work as a soloist but never got the title. And then when that shifted, I got promoted. And of course, in your mind you always think, Oh, everything goes better when I'm thinner. It's such a strange mentality, isn't it? Martin will say, "Will you stop talking about yourself in that way—you're being ridiculous." He can't stand it. But any other ballerina—same thing, the way they talk about themselves.

There's something wrong with the way, in dance, they can just up and one day say, "You know, I don't like the color of your hair. You were fabulous, and I don't like the color of your hair." I used to say to Helgi, "I get that I'm not there for you anymore at the top. And I get that you need to push these younger ones or that you have new dancers coming over from Europe." But there's a certain respect that I deserve, and I'd say, "I'll let go of this. But can we make sure I'm dancing something worthwhile?" Because it became, after a while, nothing worthwhile.

My situation there was that he loved me, and it was great even after I had Kai—I got promoted, really did well. Truthfully, some of it started going downhill around the time of the separation [from Michael]. Then, suddenly, I was having some personal issues, and then I had to fight, fight, fight…and I never really got back after that. I felt that I didn't have anything to lose. I was going to go in there and just say how I felt, because I'd really done everything I wanted to do with dance, and I just wanted to end it on a great note. It didn't work at all.

Could I have just stuck it out? Could I have pushed through? It could have been that I didn't have the temperament for that side of it. It came so naturally to me that I didn't have that part of my personality that would just fight tooth and nail to the end. Same thing with my divorce—I could have just kept fighting and fighting. But truthfully, letting go made life better for everyone. So it's hard to know: Is that my flaw? Should I have just pushed? I just wanted to be happy—I didn't need that drama in my life. When I finally started teaching, I'd come home so excited. Because I was suddenly in an environment where somebody respected me again. I quite enjoy teaching, more than I thought I ever would.

Hannah's two and a half. She holds onto our oven door and, in first, plié, relevé, plié—she's coordinated all those things. So it's hard not to go with that, because it's just fun. She's dancing. All she wants to do is put on her tutu in the house. I look back at photos of when I was very, very little, and I just loved it, and you could see that somehow.

MICHAEL LOCICERO | AUGUST 2013

We decided once Kai was born that Kristin wanted to continue dancing, and I wasn't too thrilled with the idea of working on Wall Street for the rest of my life. It was a very stressful job I had. It had taken its toll.

So I thought I needed to step up, and I thought it would be better if I raised him. I wanted to be in Kai's life 100 percent. It worked out because Kristin was so passionate about dancing—she wasn't ready to give it up. It was so much fun to be an integral part of Kai's life. I made sure Kristin saw him several times a day, so he was spending a lot of time at the ballet. Kai was surrounded by seventy new friends from all over the world. They loved him. They spent time with him. They cared for him. They were so generous with him and loving toward him. He ended up having a pretty extraordinary life. He has an intimate relationship with dance and music and how productions are put on, and he understands the discipline and the passion these dancers have. He got a chance to travel the world with the company and see the world at a very young age.

For as much as I loved being with Kai all the time, I realized that I needed to do something for myself, too. I needed to work a little bit. I had studied some bodywork in Manhattan, and I felt it was something that I was pretty good at. I started to go to school at night. If Kristin had to work while I was at school, a lot of the dancers were really great, and they would watch him backstage, or in the dressing room, or some of them might even go to the house and babysit him there.

I had been working on the dancers [at the San Francisco Ballet] because I needed bodies to work on. They got to know my work a little bit, and then it was serendipitous—there was an in-house massage therapist who quit on a Friday. It was the same day as my last class; I got certified on a Friday and hired on the Monday. The great part about it was the flexibility. My main reason to be there was Kai; when he was taking a nap or when Kristin could watch him, I could work.

I literally slept in my car for the first five days after the divorce. I rented a place in Marin for six months and several different places for six months at a time. I had nowhere to live, and I did not want to leave Kai, obviously, and Marshall [Crutcher, with Katita Waldo] took me in out of the kindness of his heart and the love for Kai, really. I went a year and a half without finding work. I'd never had a problem making money, ever. And then I went from that to nothing. I could find nothing—zero. I tried to get back into finance, and these guys would say, "Well, what did you do for these last ten years?" I told them I raised my son. Instead of seeing that as, "Wow, incredibly responsible guy, incredibly conscientious guy, someone I'd like to have here working with me," they looked at me like I was crazy.

Kai went to a prestigious school in the city, and a lot of the parents of children at that school were from the East Coast. So when it came time for him to go to high school, he and I started to research the prep schools on the East Coast, and he ended up at Middlesex. There was nothing keeping me on the West Coast, so I just decided to go back, to be closer to him, live with my sister. I see him during football season: every Saturday I go to his games and then we talk for a half hour or so and then I take off. Every once in a while we go out for dinner or something like that. I haven't missed any of his baseball games, either. So it's great. It's a bit of a trip for me. It's a two-hour drive. He started on the varsity team as a freshman.

MARTIN WEST | JUNE 2013

In 2004 I had become principal conductor at the English National Ballet. I'd had that job for six or seven months when they offered me the job [of music director and principal conductor at the San Francisco Ballet]. I was ready for a change. I was single. Life was not going in any particular direction, and I could have stayed at the National Ballet for the rest of my life, but there was nowhere else to go from there.

I came here in 2005. I started hearing that Kristin and Michael weren't that great. There was absolutely nothing between Kristin and me. She was very friendly and nice to work with, but if you're in a company of forty beautiful ballerinas, why would you even be remotely thinking of being interested in one that's married, with a kid? It was stupid. She wasn't even on my radar at all like that.

They split, and they kept the same place, so one would go there part of the week and sleep with Kai, and the other would stay with friends. I was still doing the job in England [with the English National Ballet]. I was going back for quite an extended stint, six or seven weeks. She was obviously a bit nervous about asking me, but she said, "I was wondering what you're doing with your flat while you're away?" I immediately said, "Nothing, do you want to stay? You're welcome, please."

So she did. She said, "I'll get out of your hair when you're back." I said, "Oh, that's fine. There's plenty of room." It was quite a big flat. I don't know what it was—maybe the protective nature of how I was looking after her—but it all fell into place pretty quickly. We've been together ever since.

We wanted to have children. I was pushing forty; Kristin was thirty-six—she wasn't that young. She wanted to have more children before she retired because she didn't want to retire so soon, and she didn't want to wait until forty to have children with me. And we discussed a lot with counselors what would be good for Kai. Would a child be good? Would it help him adjust? You don't know. If ever Kristin brought it up with Kai, he was dead against it—absolutely not. He was a very angry kid at that time. It was really hard for Kai. Hannah's so sweet, and now he absolutely adores her. He loves them both [Hannah and Jonah]. But it was hard for Kai when Hannah was born. And Michael was still very angry at the time.

We decided it was time, and we got pregnant absolutely immediately. [After Hannah was born] Kristin went back to work—she went straight into the gym every day. She lost all the weight pretty much straightaway. She was back in January. Her dancing was incredible, her work ethic. Halfway through that season, she was just starting to dance really well again and to be back in shape in the middle—totally kick-ass ballet. You'd never believe she'd had a child eight or nine months before. We'd just been shopping, and she walked up the stairs, and she said, "I feel so tired. What's wrong with me?" That night the cat came and sat on Kristin's tummy. We were laughing because she never does that. She sits on my tummy but not Kristin's. And we just laughed and said, "The last time she did that was when you had a nice warm belly, when Hannah was in there."

That wasn't the plan. Jonah wasn't planned then. We had it planned so that Kristin would do one more year of dancing, finish off. Then she would retire, and she'd get pregnant. That was the plan. So we had to go and tell Helgi. Then Jonah came in February. She was off all that time. But the plan was always to go back and finish off. We decided that she would go back and do one more year after that. Then when it came to it, I think Helgi wanted to be supportive, but I don't think he was entirely comfortable either, and Kristin wasn't really made to feel welcome.

It was really hard for her. Twenty-two years of amazing, dedicated work. She'd been there almost the same length of time as Helgi. The rise of the company coincided with the Kristin Longs, the Tina LeBlancs, and the Katita Waldos all arriving. That's when they started becoming a great company—when he got those young girls in, and they became amazingly true artists really early on. For Kristin it was very, very hurtful. Her retirement was largely ignored until it was too late. Everybody who leaves the ballet ends up with Tiffany earrings or something. Kristin: nothing like that.

She's very dedicated to her teaching now. When I finished the season, I was doing all of the child caring, and Kristin was teaching. Sometimes that was a lot. In July I'm going to be working quite a bit, and so is Kristin, so her mum's coming out. I've always made it my thing to take Hannah to school. And Jonah used to come with us because it was nice for Kristin to have a bit of downtime, and Jonah liked it. That can be the only time I get to spend with the kids because in the season I get up, take them to school, and then say good-bye. I'd take Jonah home, go in to work, and I might be there until 7:00 p.m. or 8:00 p.m. or 9:00 p.m. or even 11:00 p.m. On an 11:00 p.m. day generally there will be time during the day to come back for a couple of hours to see them. But on a rehearsal day, when I'm there till seven, that's it—I don't see them. Mondays, when I'm off, Kristin will be teaching. That's my day. It was very sweet. Hannah would come home. I'd say, "Let's go to the park." "No, I just want to stay here with you." Very sweet. She misses me. In the season, Sunday evening and Monday are the only times we have free, and it can get really crazy, but then the off-season kind of makes up for it. Then I'm ready to go back to work.

I don't know if having a child makes you a better dancer. But you're probably a better dancer if you're capable of having a child. You're then a different animal. You're a mother or you're a father. You've got bigger things to worry about than just dance. You do your dance in a different way. It becomes a job, and it also becomes an escape, and it also becomes something you can give to rather than something you are striving to take from. I think that's the best thing for any artist. I was desperate to be a great conductor. Having kids has changed my perspective. I realize there is more to life than only working with an orchestra.

opening image (page 25)

Cyril Pierre and Benjamin Pierce lift Kristin Long offstage. (2000)

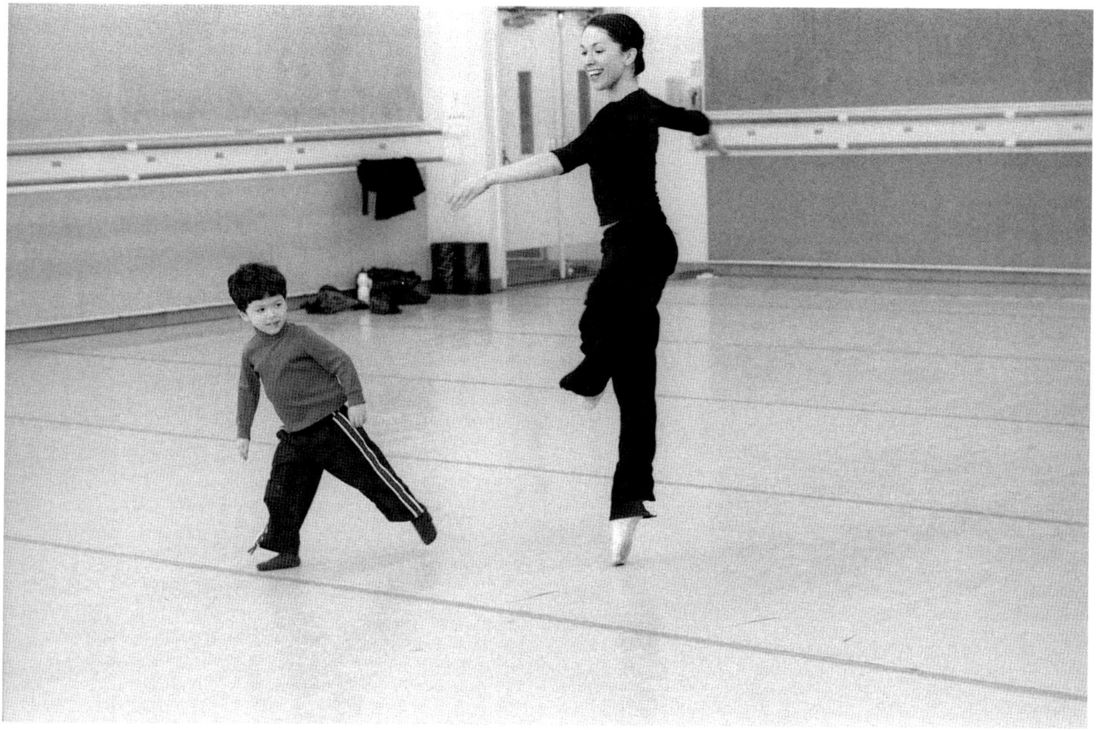

above
Kai loves to dance while his mother, Kristin, rehearses. (2000)

overleaf
Kai plays the piano with Kristin in a rehearsal room at San Francisco Ballet. He knew Chopin from Schoenberg by the time he was five; before he found baseball, it seemed as though he'd become a composer one day. (2000)

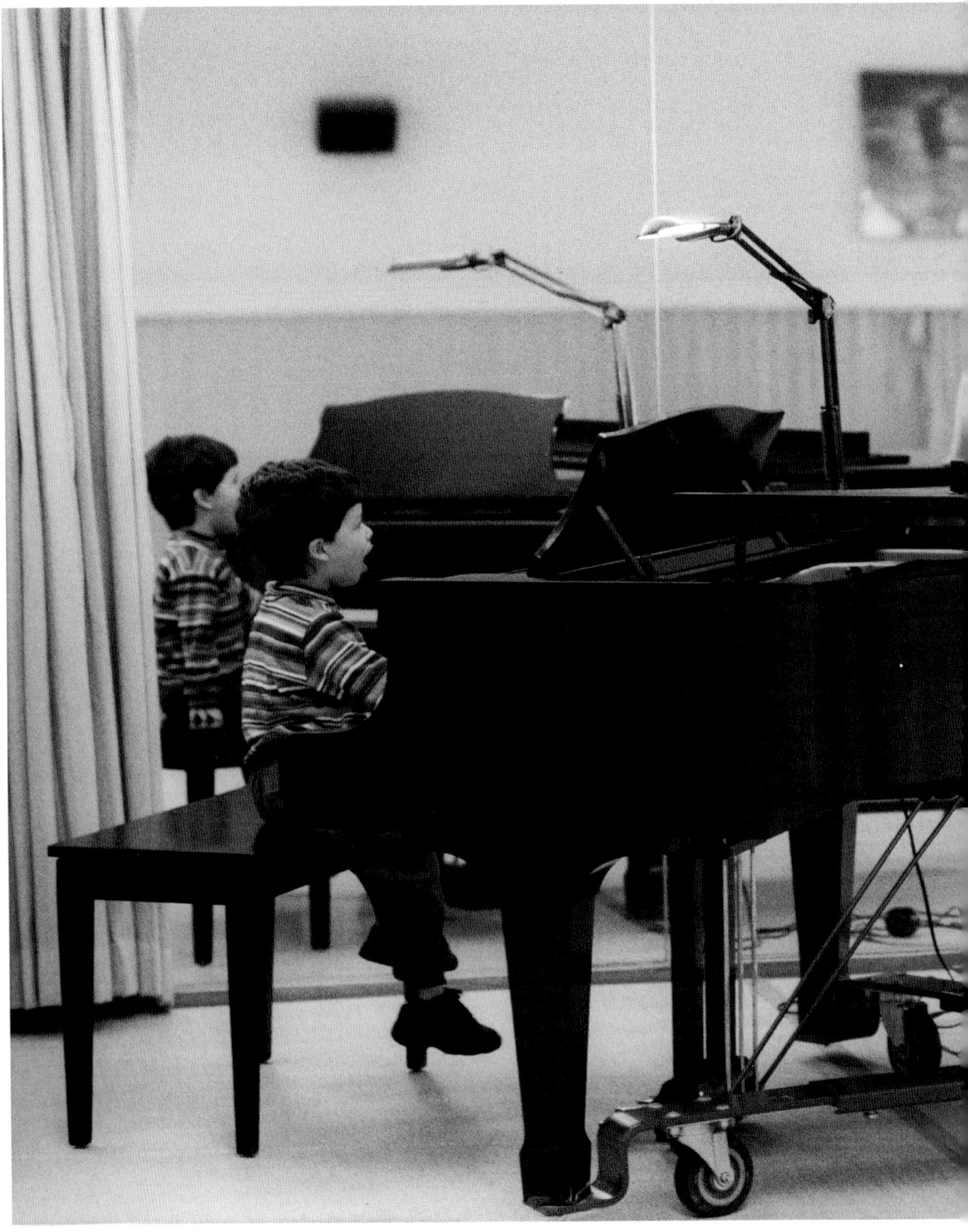

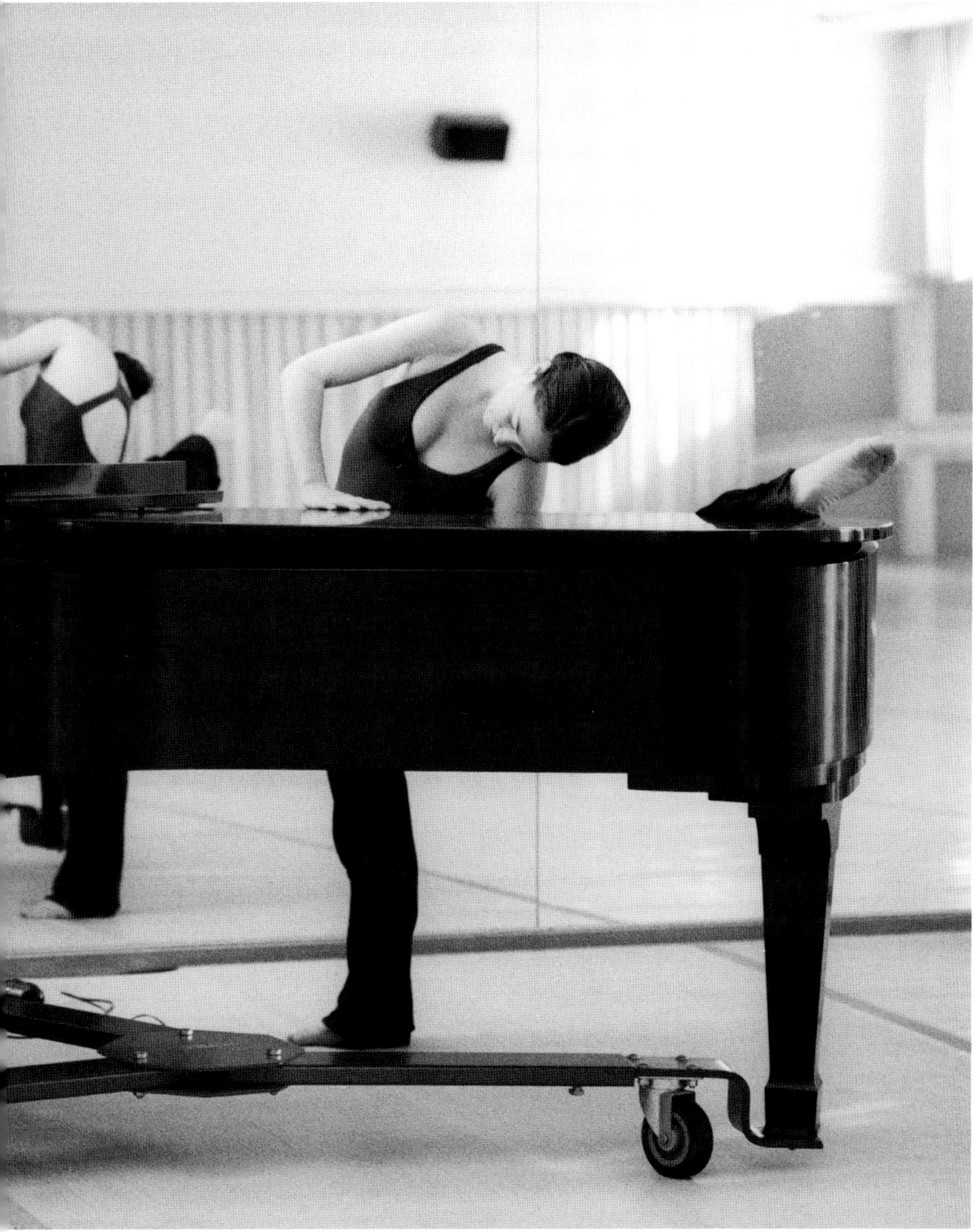

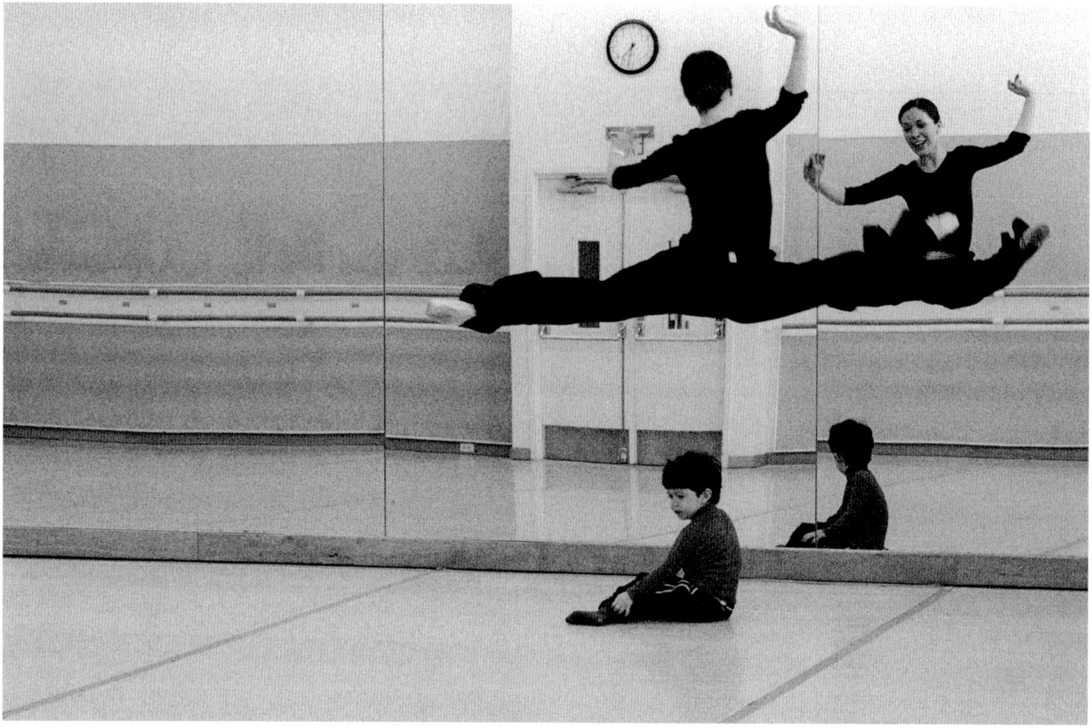

Kristin rehearses as Kai looks on. (2000)

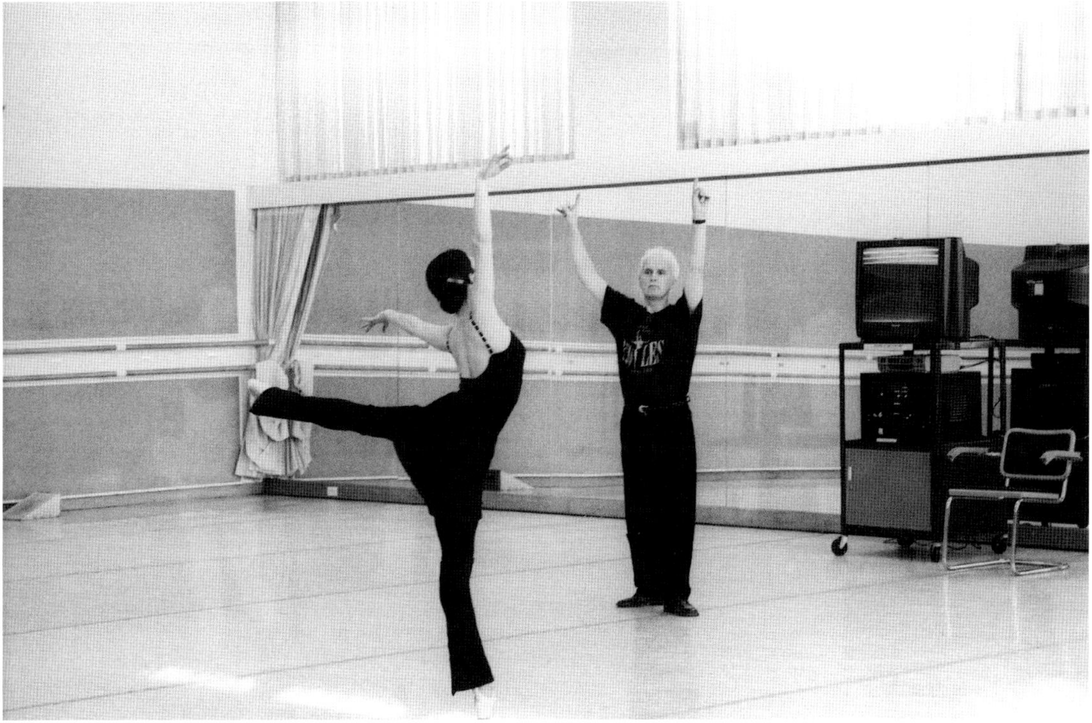

Helgi Tomasson, the artistic director of San Francisco Ballet,
rehearses Kristin for *Romeo and Juliet*. (2001)

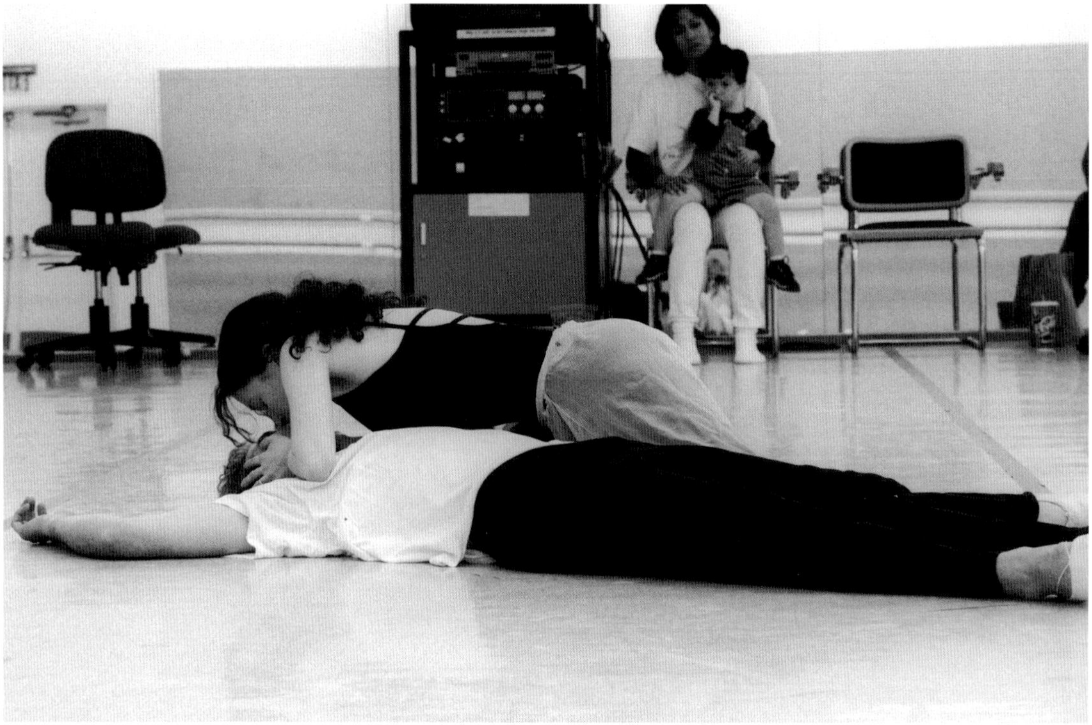

Kristin and Stephen Legate rehearse *Romeo and Juliet* (Helgi Tomasson) while Kai watches from the lap of Legate's wife, Evelyn Cisneros, an extremely popular ballerina who had retired recently from San Francisco Ballet to start a family. (2001)

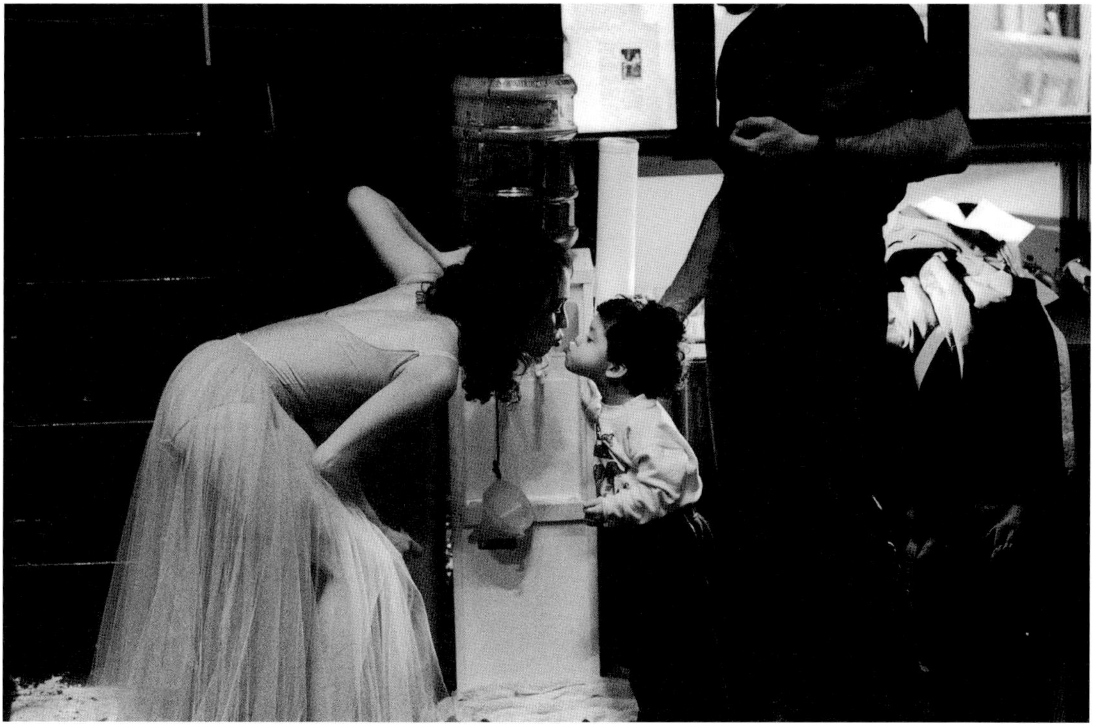

Kristin, with Kai and Michael Locicero, her first husband, before she goes onstage to perform *Symphony in C* (George Balanchine). (2001)

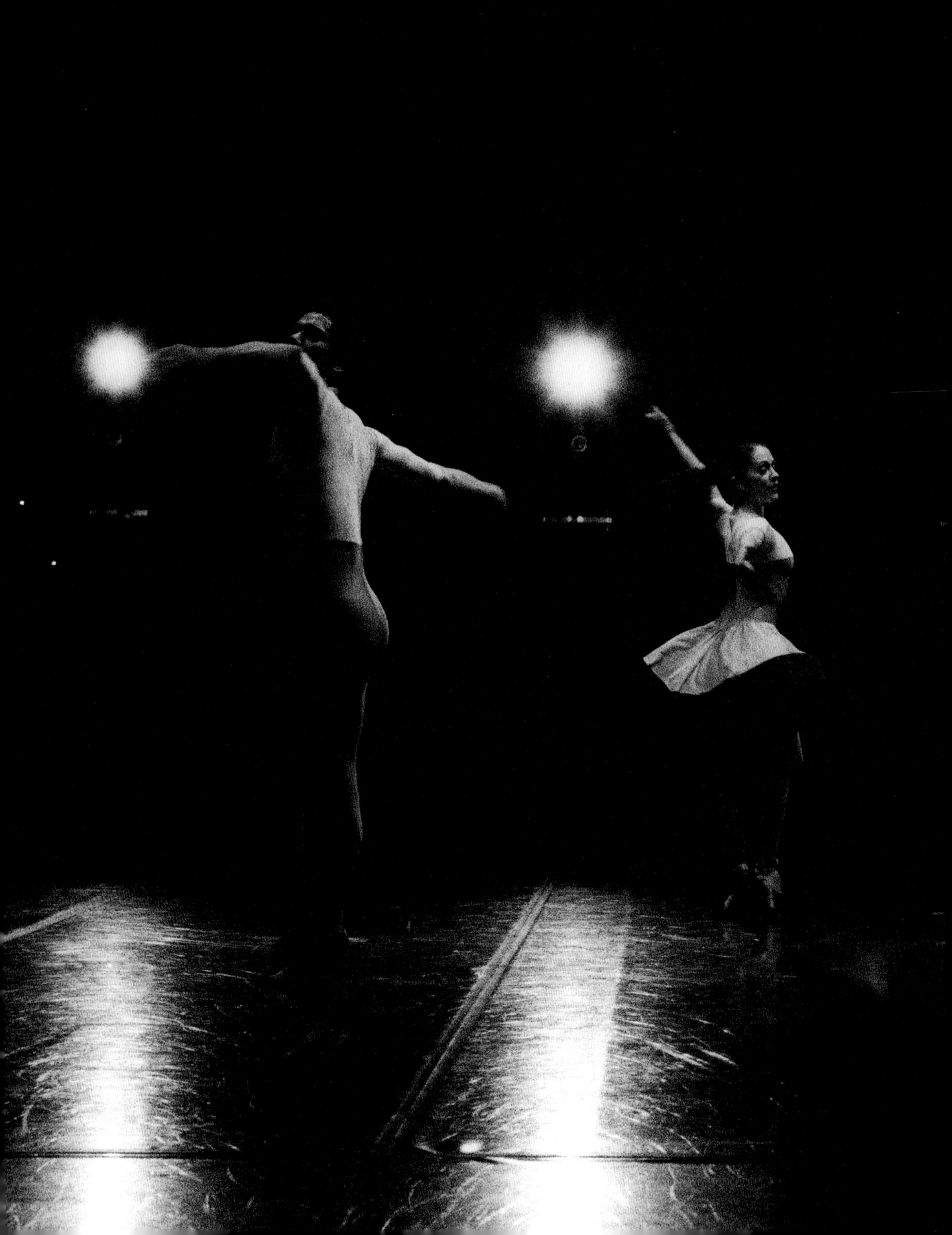

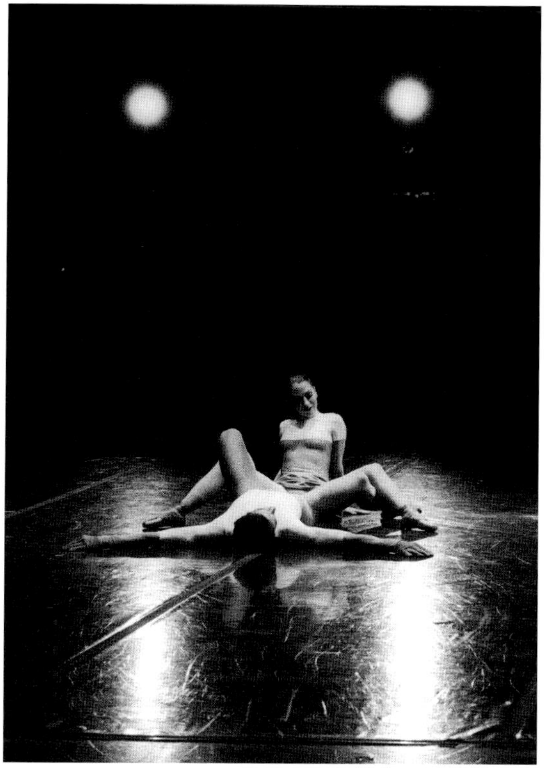

above, left, and overleaf
Damian Smith and Kristin perform
Sandpaper Ballet (Mark Morris). (2001)

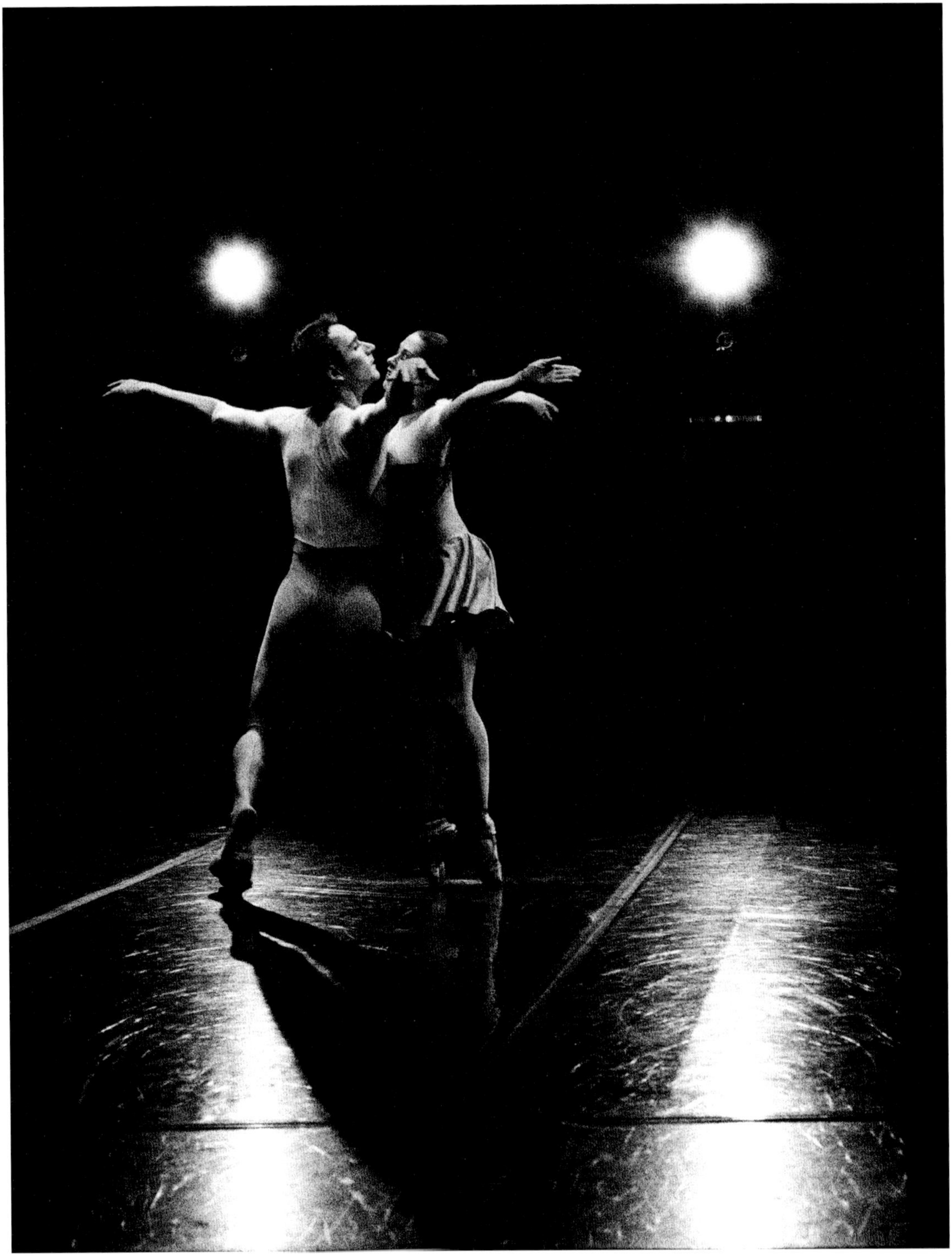

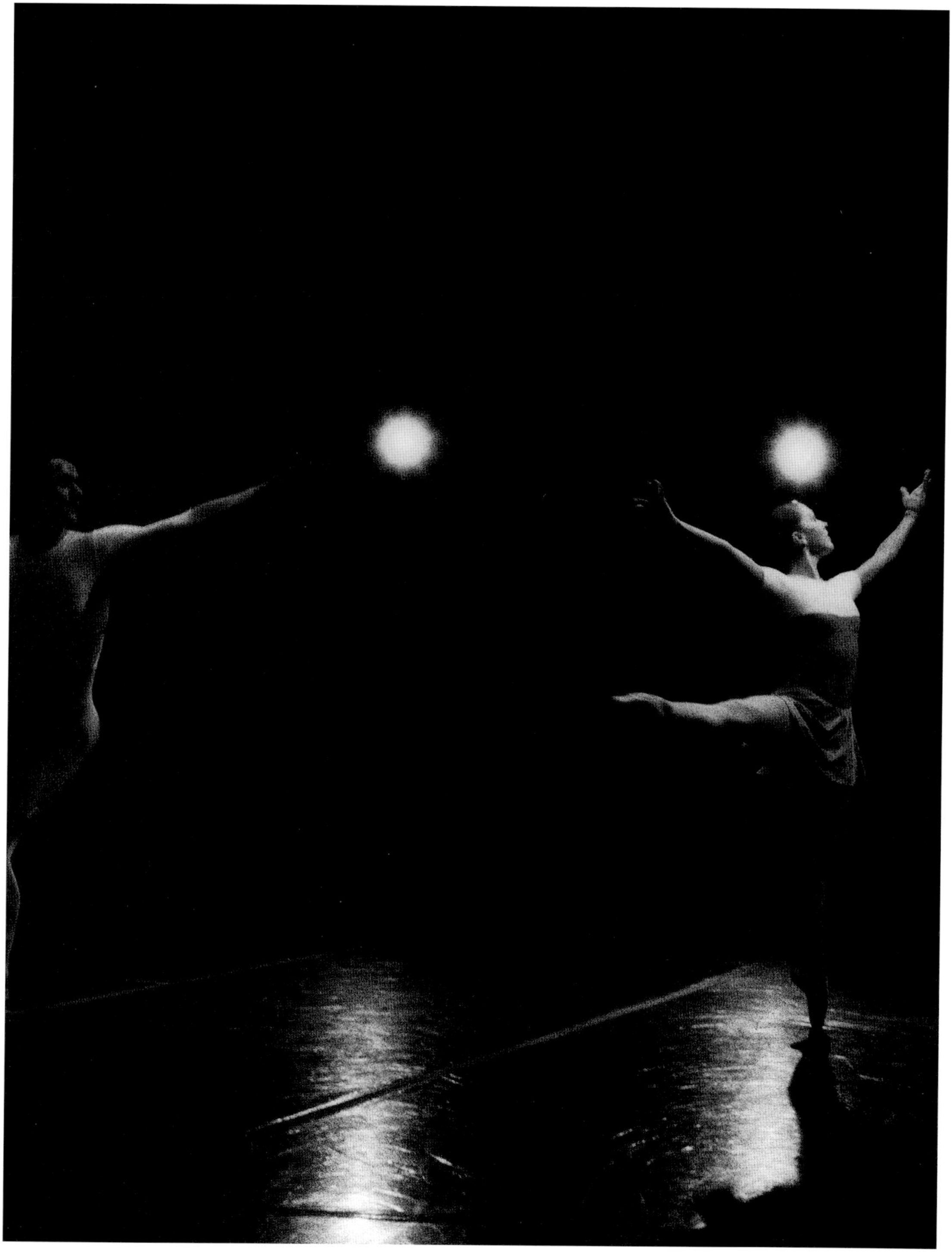

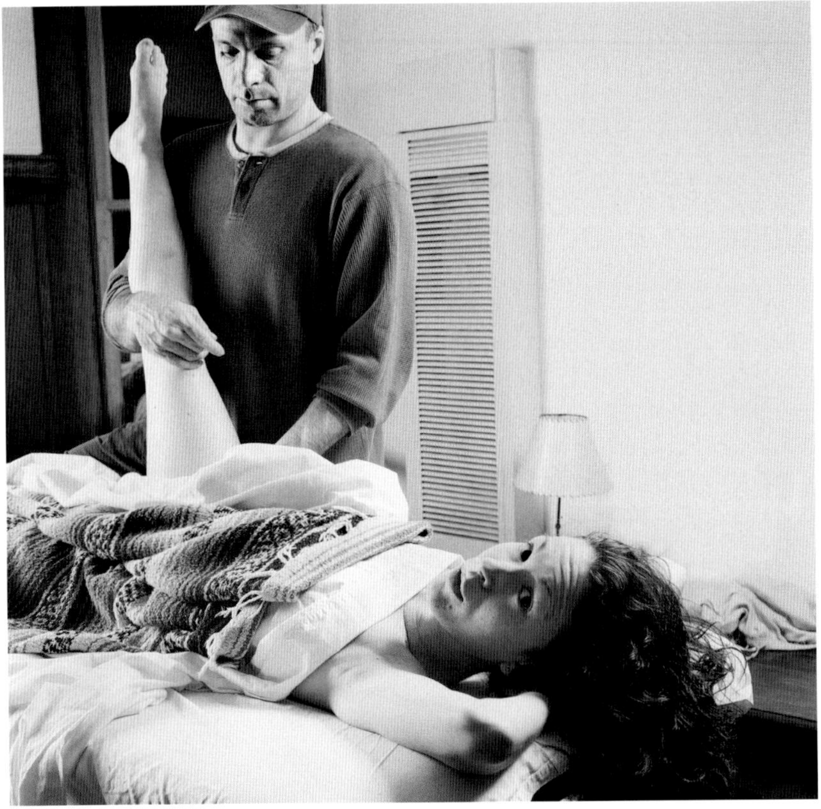

above
Michael is learning to be a massage therapist. He practices on Kristin. (2001)

right
Experiencing back trouble, Kristin goes for an MRI at California Pacific Medical Center in San Francisco. (2000)

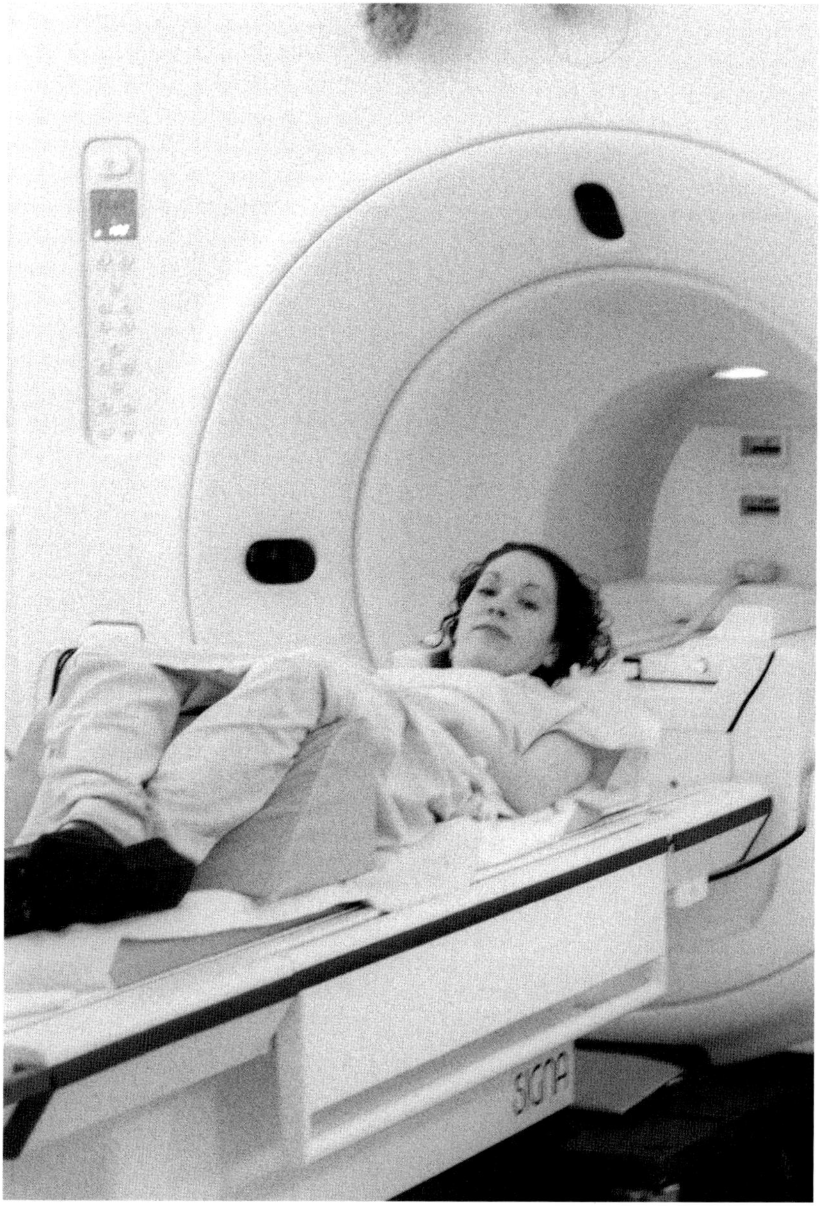
SIGNA

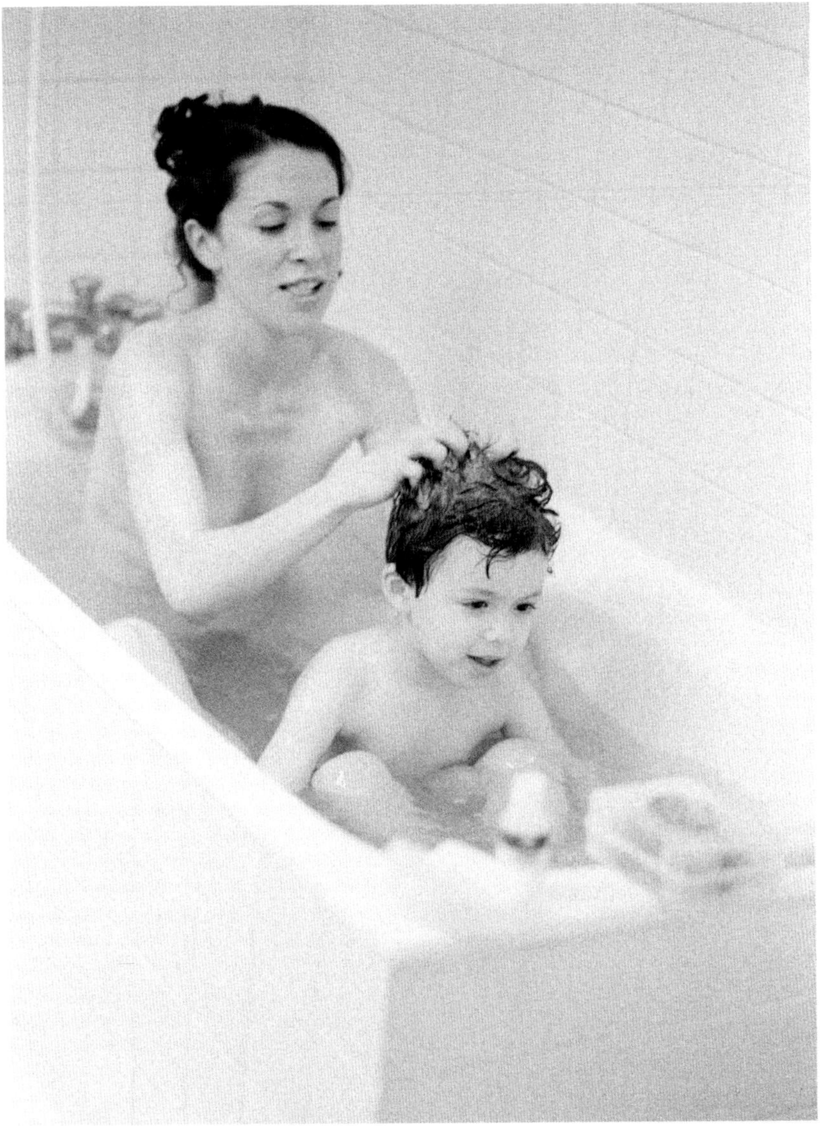

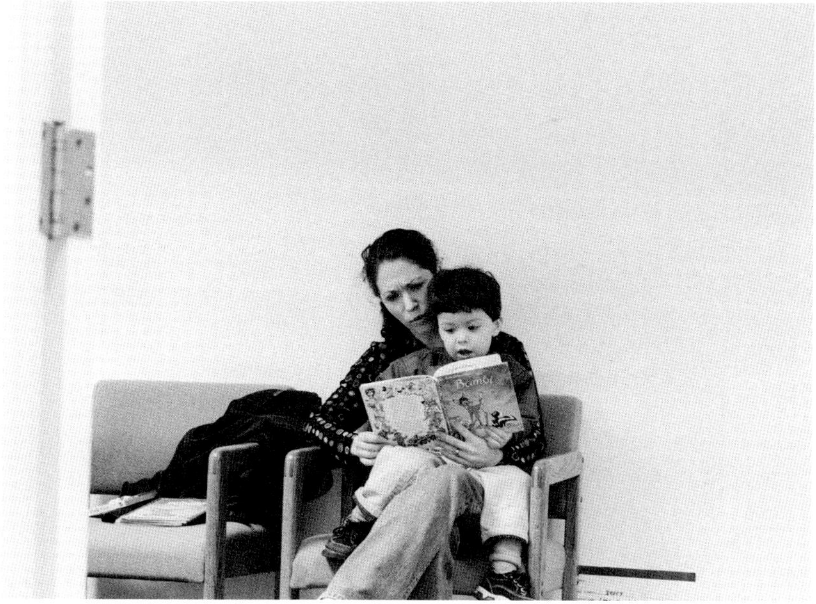

above

Kristin reads to Kai in the waiting room at her physical therapist's office in San Francisco. (2000)

left

Kristin and Kai bathe in their hotel before going to the Palais Garnier Theater in Paris, where she will perform. (2001)

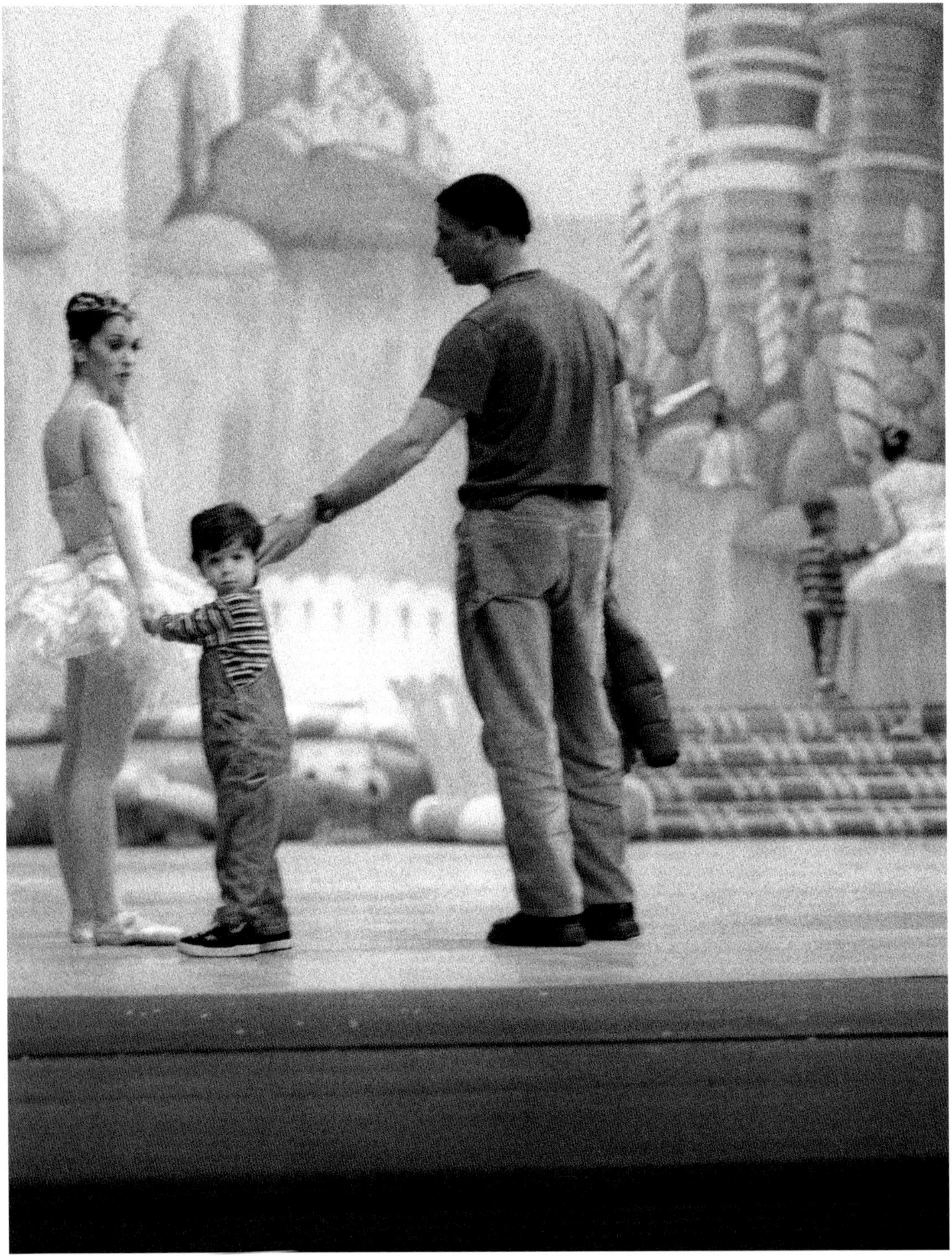

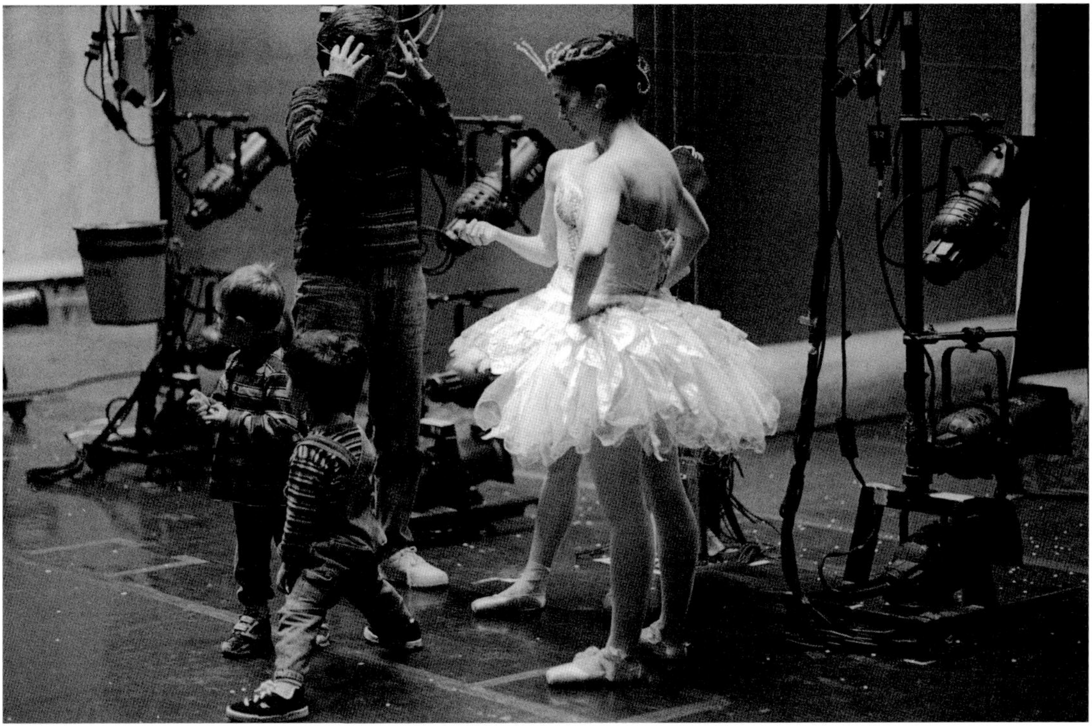

above

Tina's son Marinko; Kai (doing a split); Diane Kounalakis, the ballet's associate director of public relations; and Kristin, with Tina behind her. Kristin is brooding about her marriage. (2000)

left

After a dress rehearsal of *Nutcracker Ballet* (Marius Petipa), Kristin shows the stage to Kai and Michael. (2000)

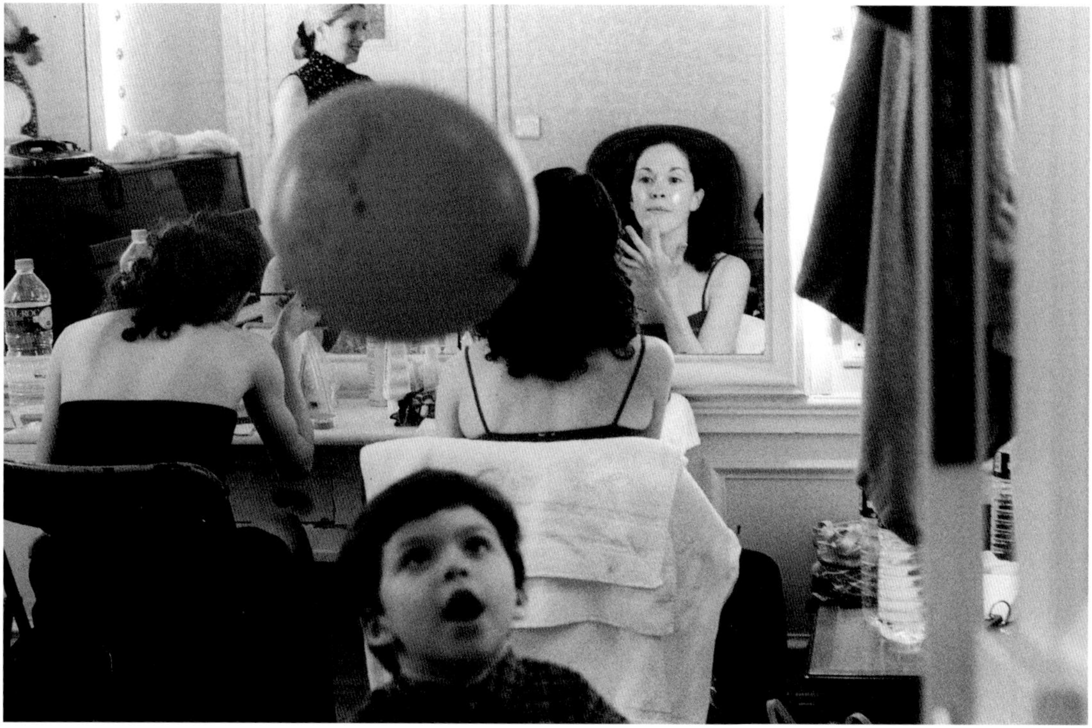

above

Before she performs, Kristin is brave enough to sneak me into her dressing room at the Palais Garnier, where no photographers are allowed. Julie Diana, with whom she shares a dressing room, does not complain. Kai hits his red balloon to his aunt, Gloria Terrell. (2001)

right

Kristin rehearses the suicide scene from *Romeo and Juliet*. She will perform this dance again in 2005, as her marriage finally dissolves. (2000)

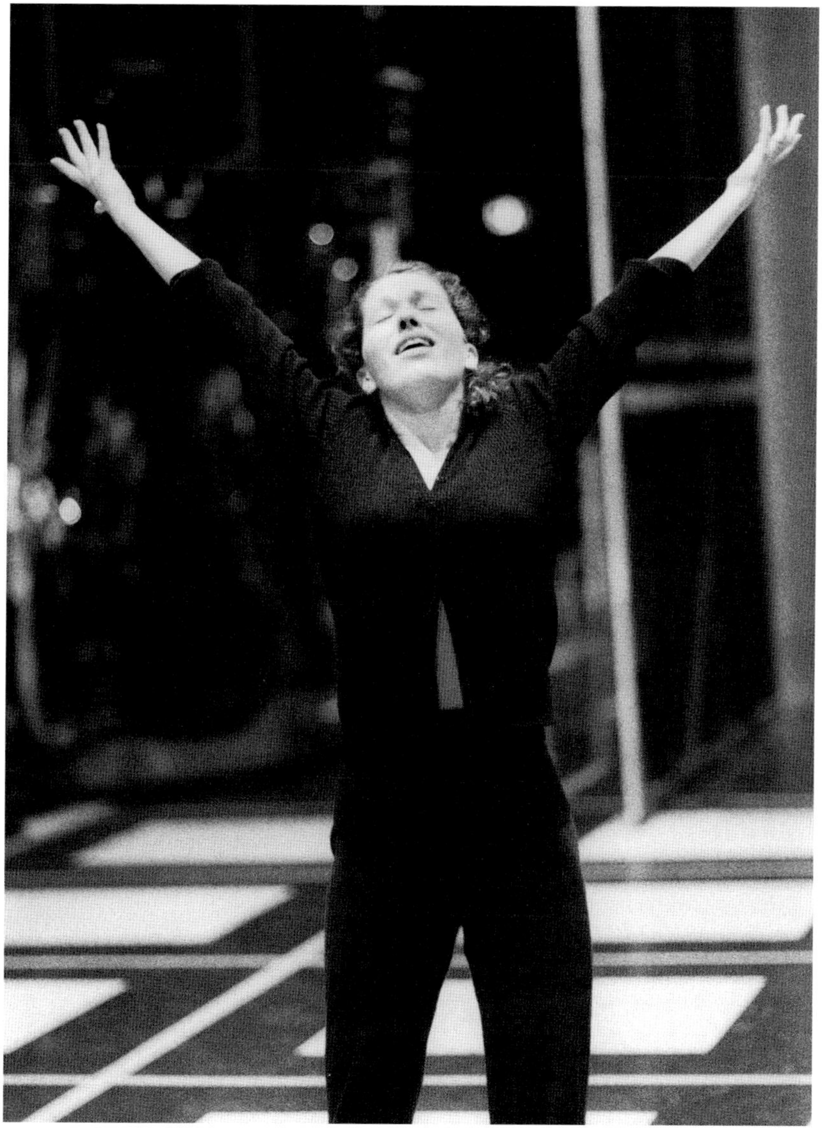

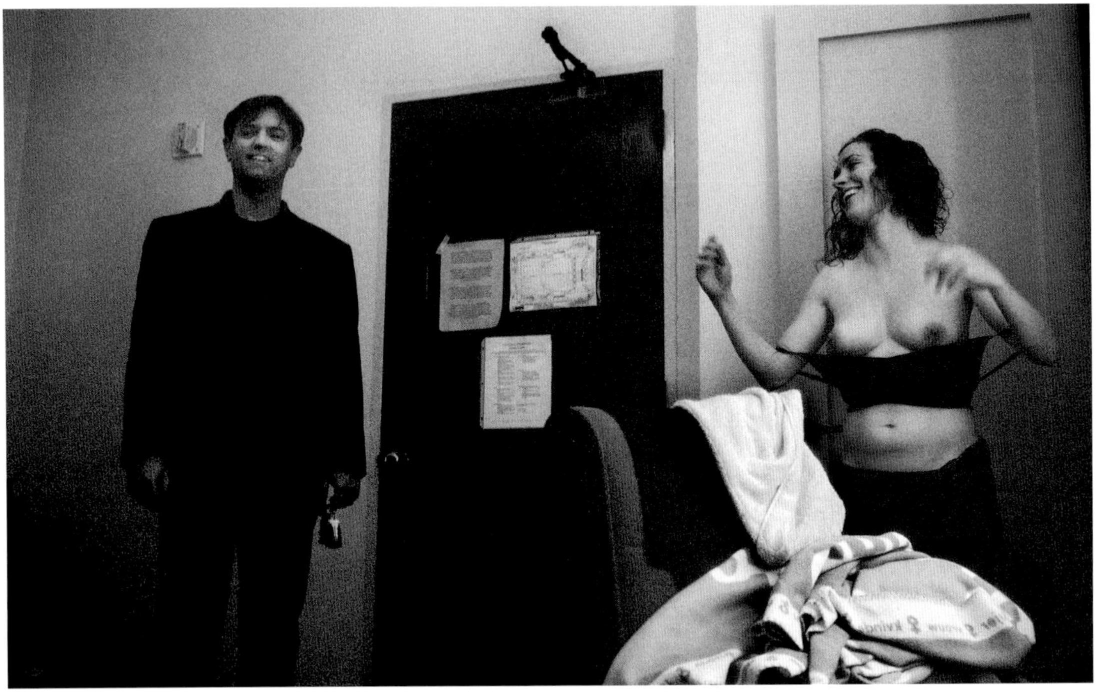

above
Martin West, the very popular music director and principal conductor at San Francisco Ballet, has become Kristin's partner. They are in Kristin's dressing room; she is three months pregnant with their daughter, Hannah. (2009)

right
Kristin is in the early phase of labor at California Pacific Medical Center's maternity ward. (2009)

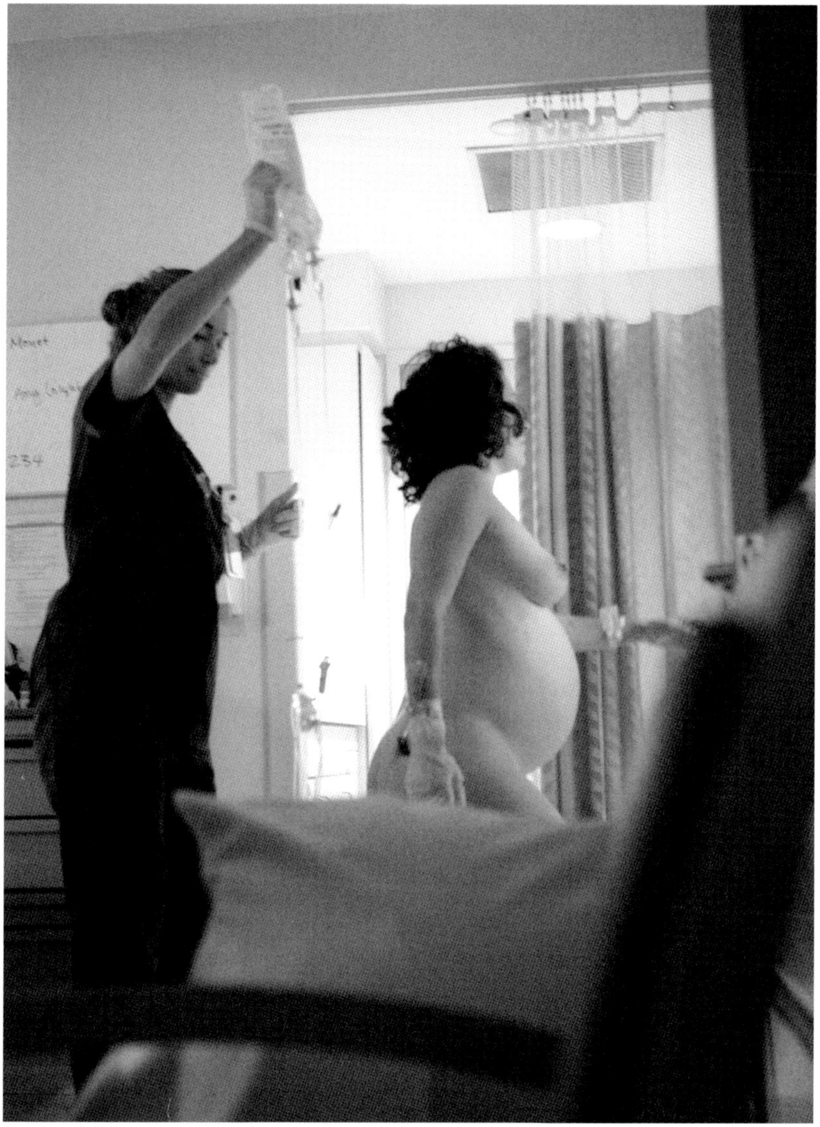

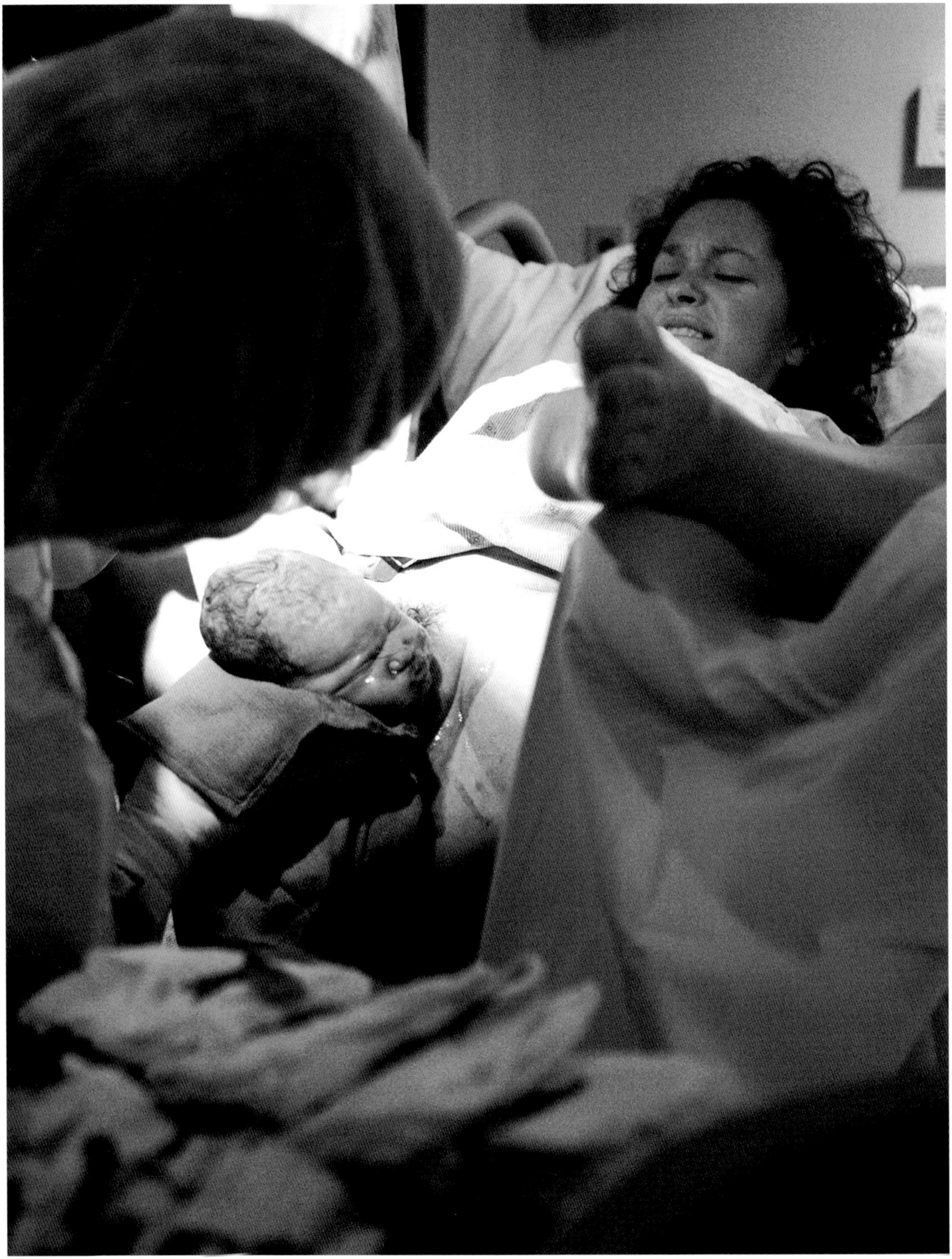

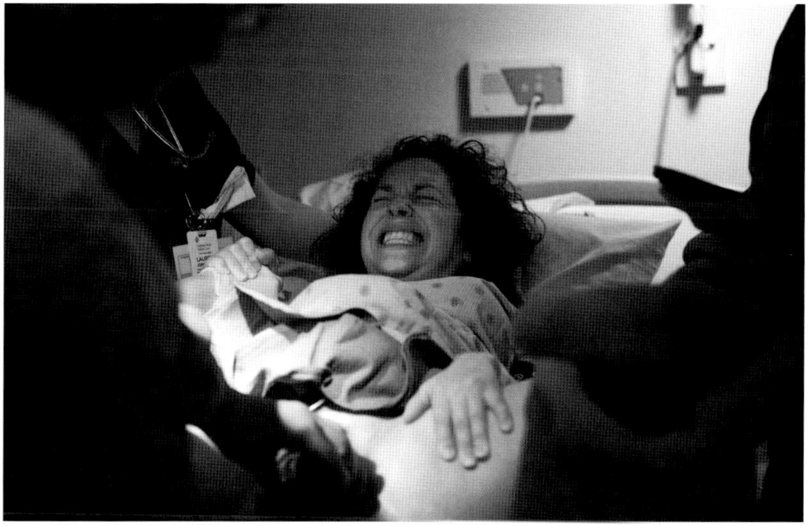

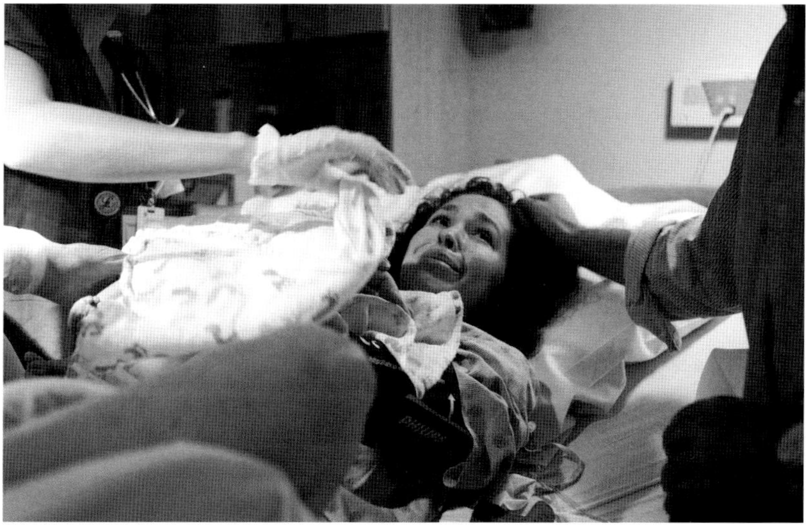

Hannah Elizabeth Long West, born after seven hours of labor on September 23, 2009.

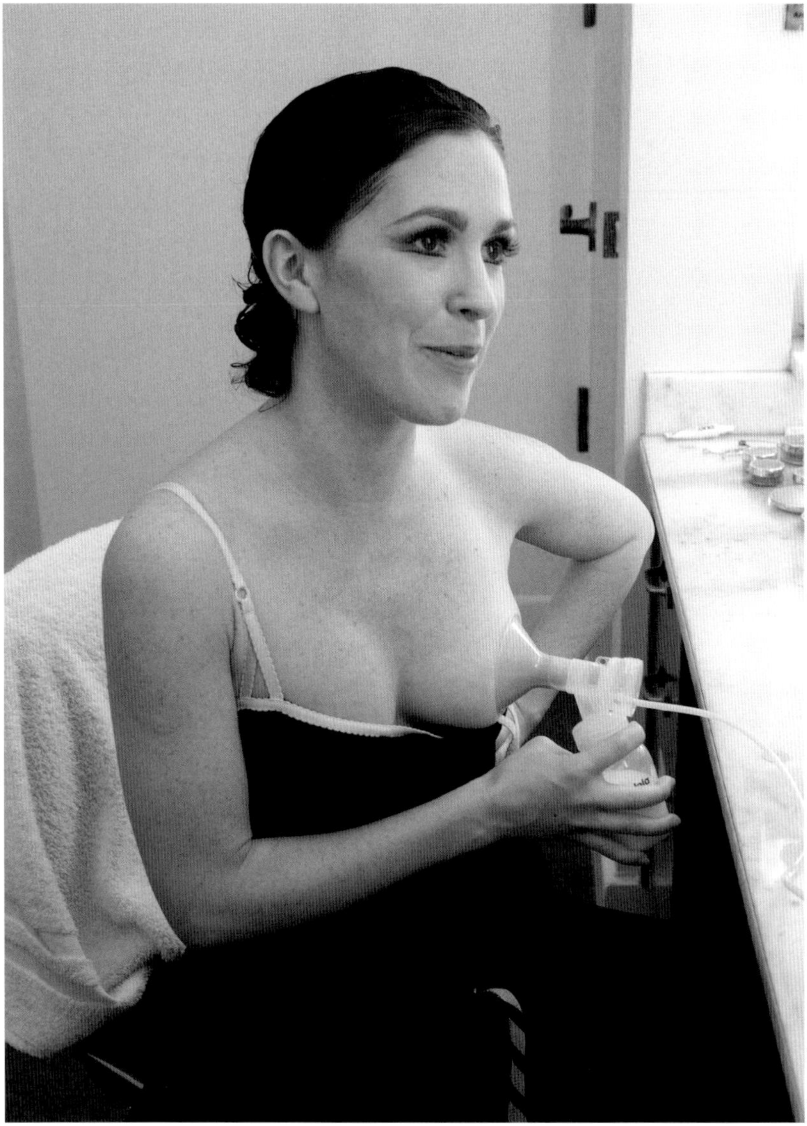

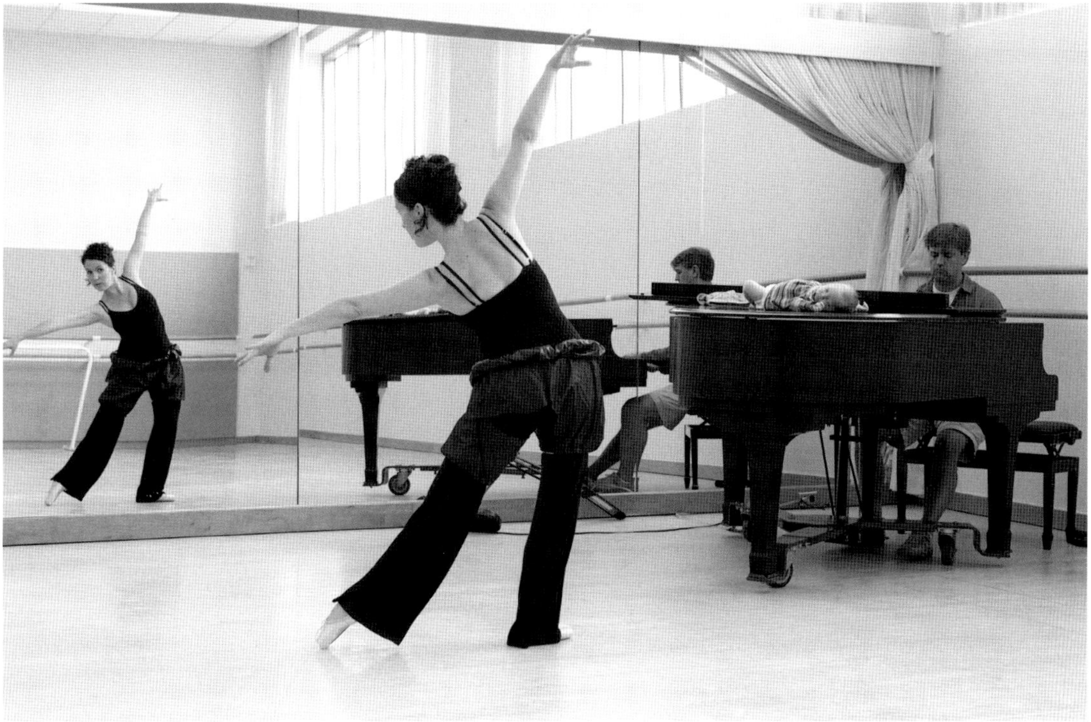

above
Kristin gets back in shape with Martin and six-week-old Hannah. (2009)

left
Kristin has received the ten-minute warning before her performance, so she pumps milk in her dressing room. (2009)

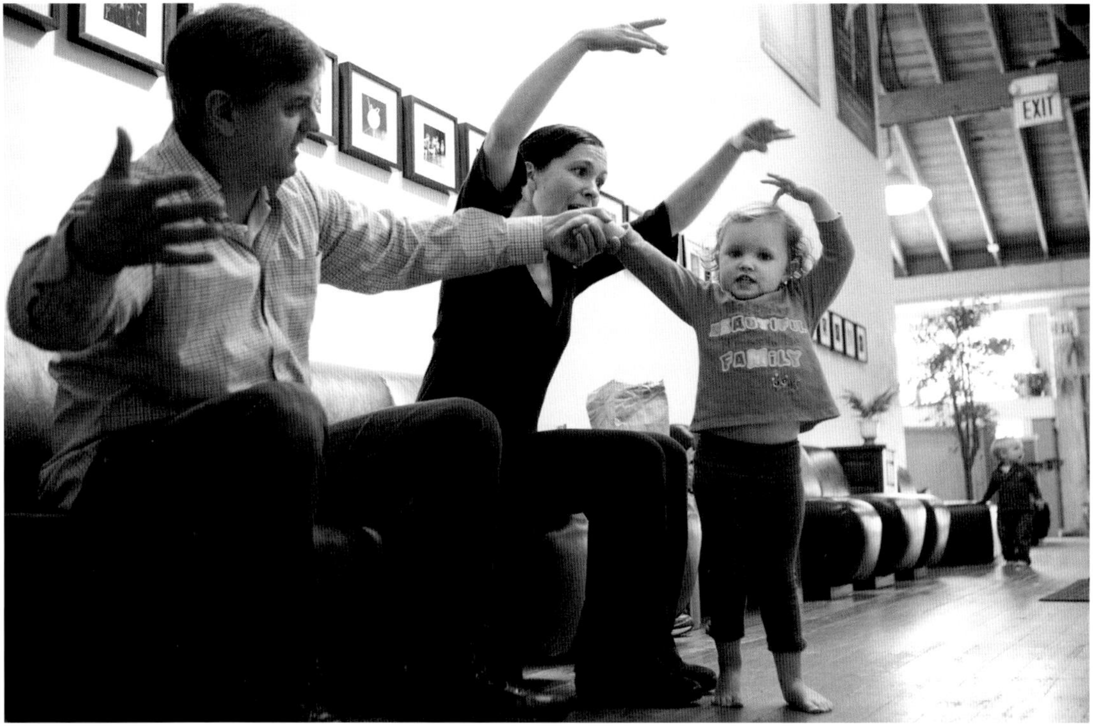

Martin; Kristin; and Hannah and her little brother, Jonah (at the end of the row of chairs), between classes at City Ballet School in San Francisco. Kristin has retired as a ballerina and teaches here. Martin is still the music director and principal conductor at SFB. (2012)

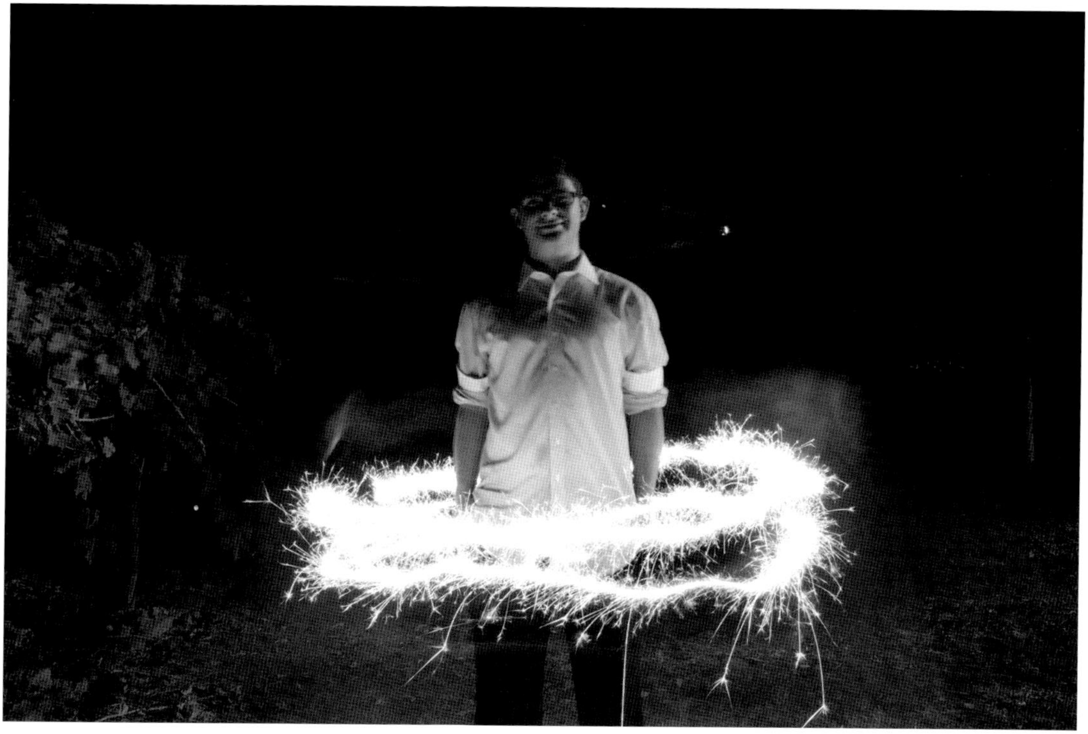

Kai, fifteen (who has just finished his freshman year of high school), on the night of his mother's wedding to Martin West. The tutu is made with sparklers. (Napa, California, 2013)

TINA LeBLANC

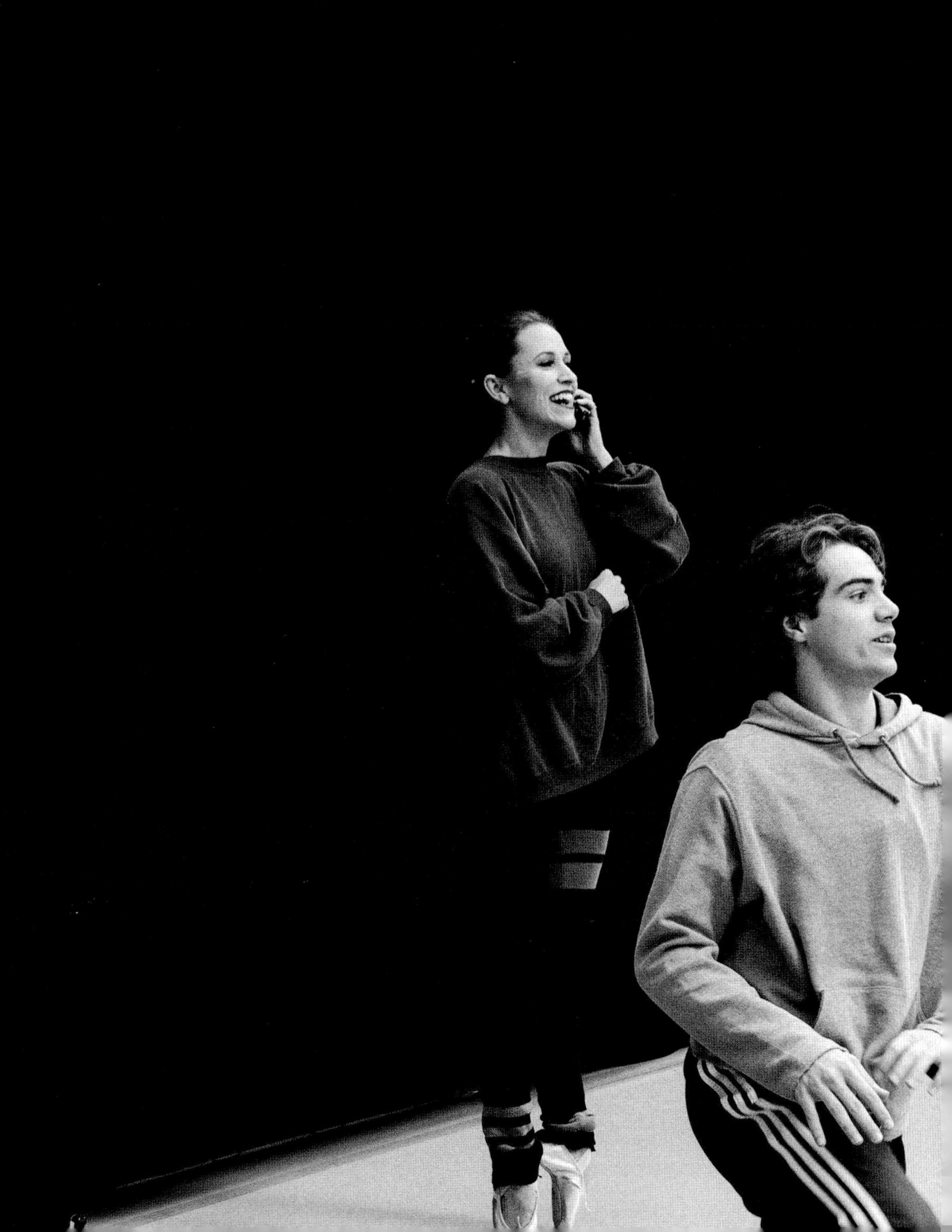

OCT 17, 1966	Born in Erie, Pennsylvania
1967	Family moves to Smyrna, Delaware, and Tina begins taking ballet classes at Marion Tracy Dance Studio in Dover
1975	Family moves to Dillsburg, Pennsylvania, and Tina begins classes at Central Pennsylvania Youth Ballet in Carlisle under Artistic Director Marcia Dale Weary
1982	Joins Joffrey II Dancers in New York City under Artistic Director Sally Bliss and Maria Grandy
1984	Invited to join Joffrey Ballet in New York City under Artistic Director Robert Joffrey and Gerald Arpino
1986	Meets Marco Jerkunica
1988	Marries Marco Jerkunica; receives first Princess Grace Statuette Award; Robert Joffrey dies, and Gerald Arpino becomes artistic director of Joffrey Ballet
1992	Joins San Francisco Ballet as a principal dancer under Artistic Director Helgi Tomasson
1995	Receives second Princess Grace Statuette Award
SEP 30, 1997	Gives birth to Marinko James Jerkunica
1998-99 SEASON	Receives first Isadora Duncan Dance Award
2000-01 SEASON	Receives second Isadora Duncan Dance Award
FEB 1, 2003	Gives birth to Sasha Johan Jerkunica
2009	Retires from San Francisco Ballet and joins the faculty at the San Francisco Ballet School

TINA LeBLANC | APRIL 2002

My father was a salesman of very many things. He came from a family that was in vaudeville. His father and brother and sister were tappers, soft-shoe and stuff, and he was the singer. He had a beautiful voice. He loved to ballroom dance, and my mom did not like dancing. She started out as a registered nurse and then went on to become a nurse-anesthetist. They're both retired now.

I have two sisters and a brother. All the girls dance professionally. My brother took dance in Delaware. Then we moved to Pennsylvania when I was about eight, and at that point, my brother said, "That's enough for me."

By the age of twelve I was doing fifteen classes a week, in addition to school. I studied at the Marcia Dale Weary Dance School, now called the Central Pennsylvania Youth Ballet. We were there six days a week—Saturdays, all day. I know—it was crazy! But the ballet school was where all of my social relationships were. I was a mouse at school, a total wallflower. I only did two years of high school and then left for New York. I did the rest by correspondence.

When I was fourteen I auditioned for the School of American Ballet and American Ballet Theatre summer programs. I was accepted to both. The ABT audition was a cattle call—so many people. Three of us were kept. I ended up doing the SAB summer course and then following it with two weeks at ABT.

The second year I auditioned for ABT's summer program, cattle call again. Again, I see that I am one of the best dancers in the class—there's never any doubt in my mind. They've cut people all along, and toward the end of the class—the very last cut—they said, "OK, these people stay." I was confused at first. I thought, Did I miss it? I couldn't believe it. One of the ladies running the audition knew me. She called me up and said, "You know what it is, don't you?" And I said no, but, of course, the first thing that popped into my head was, I'm too fat. And she said, "You're just too short. Right now Mikhail Baryshnikov is only looking for tall people." (I did go through a very round stage. But it wasn't then; it hit more along the lines of sixteen–seventeen through twenty-one–twenty-two, when I was filling out.)

It crushed me because ABT was the only place I had ever wanted to go. That was my dream. It was a real blow to my motivation at that point. Those few months when I didn't know where I was going to go, I was lost.

Then we did a regional festival. Our company was hosting that year. I did the lead in this piece. We brought the house down—they went crazy. My mom came back after the show and said, "The director of Joffrey II [the apprentice company of the Joffrey Ballet] is out there, and she wants to talk to you." I didn't know anything about the Joffrey. My mom took me over to this table, and this very large woman jumped out of her chair and said "Tina!" and hugged me. As it turned out, I loved her to pieces. She said that she and her codirector had been watching me develop through the years, and they wanted me to join Joffrey II.

My circle of friends was always at the ballet. I didn't have many boyfriends. I met Marco (who was a dancer, but not professionally) through a friend at the Joffrey. He had danced regionally in Laguna Beach, California. He had come to New York to help a friend of his build a theater, supposedly for three months, and stayed for eight years. The theater never materialized. They started their own construction team.

After he was in construction for eight years in New York, he said, "Get me out of here before I go insane." That was one of the reasons we came out to San Francisco. I had been with the Joffrey for almost ten years, and I was feeling a bit smothered, feeling a bit like I knew exactly what my role was in the company. I needed new energy. I needed new everything.

I came to the San Francisco Ballet as a principal, so I have a slightly different relationship with Helgi than someone who came up through the ranks. He might deny it. I'm sure there are things about my dancing that he doesn't like, because it's all a matter of taste, but he didn't watch me develop. Some people he just won't let grow up: he won't acknowledge that they have outgrown a certain thing or that they've improved in a certain way.

Kristin and I have the fortunate-but-unfortunate thing of being small, strong, and fast. So we will get those roles over the ballerina roles. You look at *Symphony in C*: the first movement calls for the quintessential bubbly ballerina. The second one is for the adagio ballerina. The third is the sprite. We will always do the sprite. Not that we can't do the first one but because not many people can do the third one, whereas a lot more people can attempt the first one.

I hadn't necessarily planned to marry young [at twenty-one] but always, from the time I was a child, I knew I wanted kids. And from the time I was a child, I said I was going to have my first child before I was thirty and then go back to dancing. (I almost made it—I had Marinko a month before my thirty-first birthday.) It didn't seem illogical at all to ask that of myself, because so many ladies go back to work. Why couldn't I?

When I told Helgi I was pregnant, Kristin had been out with a broken foot. She was in New York recuperating, and Michael was living there. She got pregnant. She came back, and she had a meeting with Helgi. When I saw her, I had just found out I was pregnant. But I had been working on it—mine was planned.

This was a week before the Opening Night Gala. The day after the Gala, I walked in there and said, "I'm pregnant." He didn't say anything. I said, "Of course, I'll dance as long as I can. And I fully intend to come back, as soon as I can." I just kept talking, because he wasn't saying anything. Finally, he said, "Is this what you want?" And I said, "Yes." And he said, "Then I'm happy for you." He's a dad, too. (Maybe not as hands-on as some, but....) After a minute, it hit him that he had no more small dancers. In that respect it was kind of good because Kristin and I both came back and filled in the roles that had been missing, for the small, strong, fast female dancers. It was nice for us to be able to step back into that.

There is a part of me that would like to be a stay-at-home mom. However, I have a wonderful career that gives me expression, and I'm not ready to give that up. Also, I think I appreciate my time with my son more because it's quality time. I know I don't have much of it, so I make the best of it. I still get frustrated—I am an impatient person—but I can bring myself wholly to it.

I think you'll find that the reason so many dancers are a little nuts is because they aren't fulfilled. They haven't made it to where they want, because someone else is in control of their career. To a certain extent, you are responsible for yourself—how you act, how you apply yourself, how open you are to criticism—but, essentially, it comes down to whether the director gives you that part or promotes you. And if you don't get to where you make peace with that, it can mess you up. It can make you bitter; it can change your outlook.

TINA LeBLANC | SEPTEMBER 2002

In the sixth week after Marinko was born, I started back with my own class, just to get moving again. I wanted to start really slowly and just do bar. The first thing up was *Nutcracker*, and then in January there was the Gala—the first Gala after the Opera House was renovated. It was going to be a huge deal. I knew that I would be included in it, and I knew they would have me do something hard because they always do. I thought that would be terrifying, all that pressure first time back after having a baby, so I was determined to dance in some shows of *Nutcracker*, just to get my stage feet back. I'm glad I did. It was something that was familiar; it wasn't too difficult, and there wasn't a lot of pressure. I had a couple of decent shows, and I had a couple of bad ones, but it let me know where I was at. I was probably a little heavy, but it worked out the best for me.

This time around I will have the baby in the beginning of February, and the end of the season is the beginning of May. It may take a little longer the second time—you never know. I'll take the rest of the season and be with my baby and then worry about getting into shape. I'll start back in July, when the company starts back. And hopefully I'll be closer to being in shape by then.

The first time, even performing and working, it took me five months to get to a decent weight. It wasn't like I had a lot to work off. Two weeks after Marinko was born, I was only ten pounds heavier, because he was so big. It took me five months to lose those ten pounds. I remember hitting a point where it seemed like nothing would get the weight off. I was working, I had stopped breast-feeding, and I hit a wall. I just couldn't lose weight. Then, after a couple of weeks, the body kicked in.

I really feel that being a more well-rounded person helps me understand roles and keeps a perspective on what I'm doing. OK, I'm nervous for this performance, but I'm not saving a life, am I? I'm out there entertaining people. Who cares if I slip and fall down? It's a personal challenge. It's not their judgment that I should be worried about.

When I came back after having Marinko, I felt so different as a dancer. No longer was it my live-or-die sort of thing. It was fun. My work was at home—that was my job. My priority was to raise this little being and enjoy that. In the beginning, coming back to work was my quiet time. I was comfortable with it, and I could leave home, where I would be thinking, "Oh, my God, what's he doing? Oh, it's not supposed to be this way!" First-time-mom stuff. I found it beneficial to both [my work and my family].

For the first months I took Marinko in to the artistic staff at the ballet, and they took care of him while I would take class and rehearse. I said, "I'd really like to come back. I'd really like to do this. But if you want me, I'm going to need help," and they were willing to take that step. I was the first one. Kai was older, but Kristin wasn't back. She had been out injured, and she came back the following year, so her baby was already nine months old. I was really lucky; I don't think they'd be that tolerant now.

Whether or not Marinko takes ballet classes, whether or not he becomes a dancer, he will at least have had that incredibly special experience of being around the theater. I think one day he will appreciate that. I am hoping because I think it's an amazing thing.

MARCO JERKUNICA | JULY 2013

I met Tina in 1986. She's shy, she's nineteen. I'm seven years older than her. We went out on a date, and I kissed her at the bowling alley. She was taking score, and I couldn't resist! And she kicked my ass in bowling. More than a year went by before we started dating. We were engaged within a year, in July 1987. Then we got married in May of '88. One year—maybe the second year we were married—they toured for almost *nine months*! So a lot happens on the road, or could happen on the road. You're in a field where people are trying to pick up your wife all the time. You're trying to keep this sense of normalcy in an almost impossible situation. I've sat in the audiences—and the comments I've heard over the years.... I've given her publicness—I've accepted that gracefully. I had wanted kids much earlier. There have been a few bumps with us, and this was one of them. She traveled too much with the Joffrey [to have children]. So we moved, but Tina said, "No, I just got in the San Francisco Ballet company."

I started a contracting company with two guys, one I met through SFB. I was with them for five years. Then I got dialed in to this stagehand thing for almost ten years. I over romanticized it. It ended with [the television series] *Nash Bridges*. So I started my own company again. That's what I do. It's been great because I actually get time with the kids.

Tina did the morning routine because I'm always leaving home at six-thirty, seven o'clock, and class didn't start until late for her. Fortunately, our nanny lives a three-minute walk from here. We've always had dinner together whenever possible. I mean *always*. The thing that was nice about Tina being a principal was that she wasn't on every night. So we had those nights of being a family.

I do most of the cooking. Tina probably does 75 percent of the housework. I do dishes. She does vacuuming. She does dusting. Tina does the laundry. I do a lot of it, but she does most of the folding. I cannot do origami folding like she does—it fits in the drawers when she does it.

It was easier when Tina was dancing than it is now because her schedule is six days a week, guaranteed. When she was dancing, there would be two or three days when she didn't have rehearsal. She'd just go in and take class. But that's just the way it is now. Just one day off. It's tough. We're totally struggling. And work has been slow in construction. But we were luckier than Katita and Marshall. We bought our house in '94 for $235,000. Property values were going up, and I did the improvements. We couldn't rent for what we have here. But we're OK, I think. We're over the shock of that transition.

Somebody had to be flexible. It's as simple as that. There were so many things that happened along the way where I just had no say, and there was no flexibility, particularly after kids. I'm not going to leave my kid with a nanny all the time—that's just not going to happen. And our marriage survived, which is still unusual in this field. You don't have a twenty-five-year marriage alone, in a vacuum. Her kids were well taken care of, her needs were taken care of, her cars ran. I supported her. I didn't smother her with jealousy. I'm not a Backstage Johnny. Most of the husbands who aren't dancers are always there. To me, that was hers.

TINA LeBLANC | JULY 2013

I was always thinking about teaching, so I am not surprised that teaching was in my future. I feel lucky that I have been able to stay with San Francisco Ballet. This organization has a great facility, and beautiful dancers come our way.

There are definitely certain aspects of performing that I miss. I miss the self-focus. I miss the downtime before a show, when you're getting into your character and getting ready. I miss the excitement right before you go onstage. Pointe shoes, I do miss them. I miss the feeling of energy going through my toes, being able to stand right up on top. The feeling of, say, turning on pointe or hitting a balance, where there's absolutely nothing but your energy pushing into the earth. There's only your toes to balance on, there can't be any wobbling, you've got to be right up there on the top. It's an amazing feeling. I miss that thrill when you feel you've done well. I miss that whole process. I don't miss the daily grind of having to push myself—not only mentally but

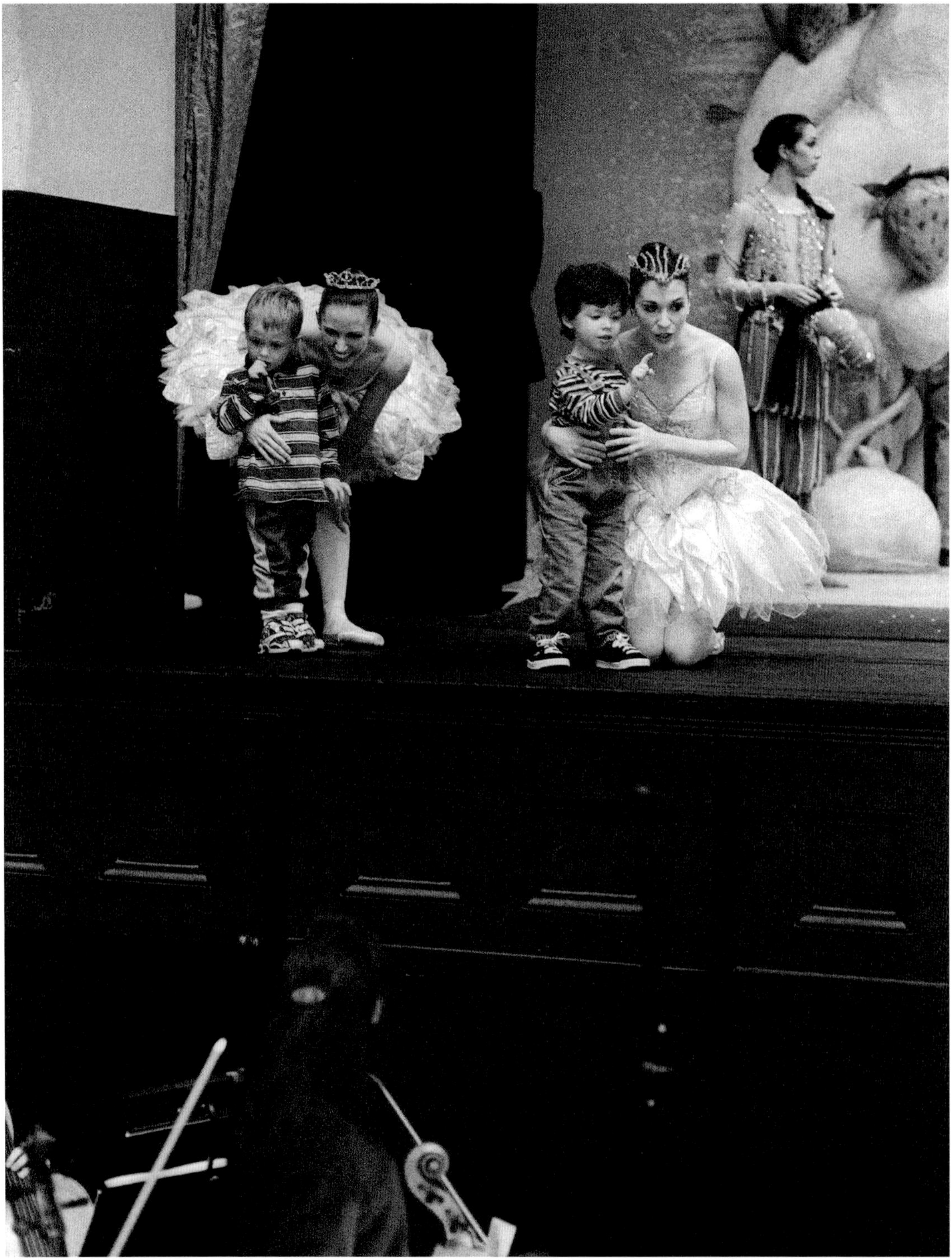

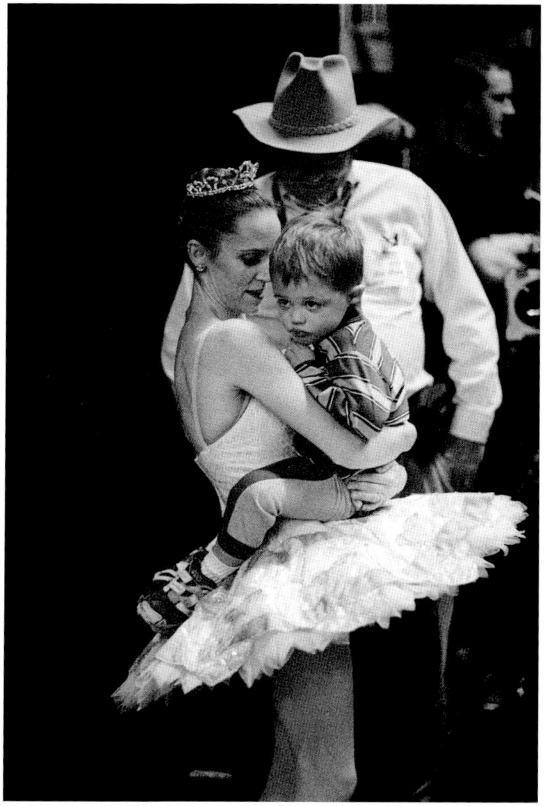

above
Marinko is shy. Tina holds him, backstage after a performance of *Nutcracker Ballet* (Marius Petipa). A patron of the ballet looks on. (2000)

left
Tina and Kristin show their children the orchestra pit of the War Memorial Opera House. (2000)

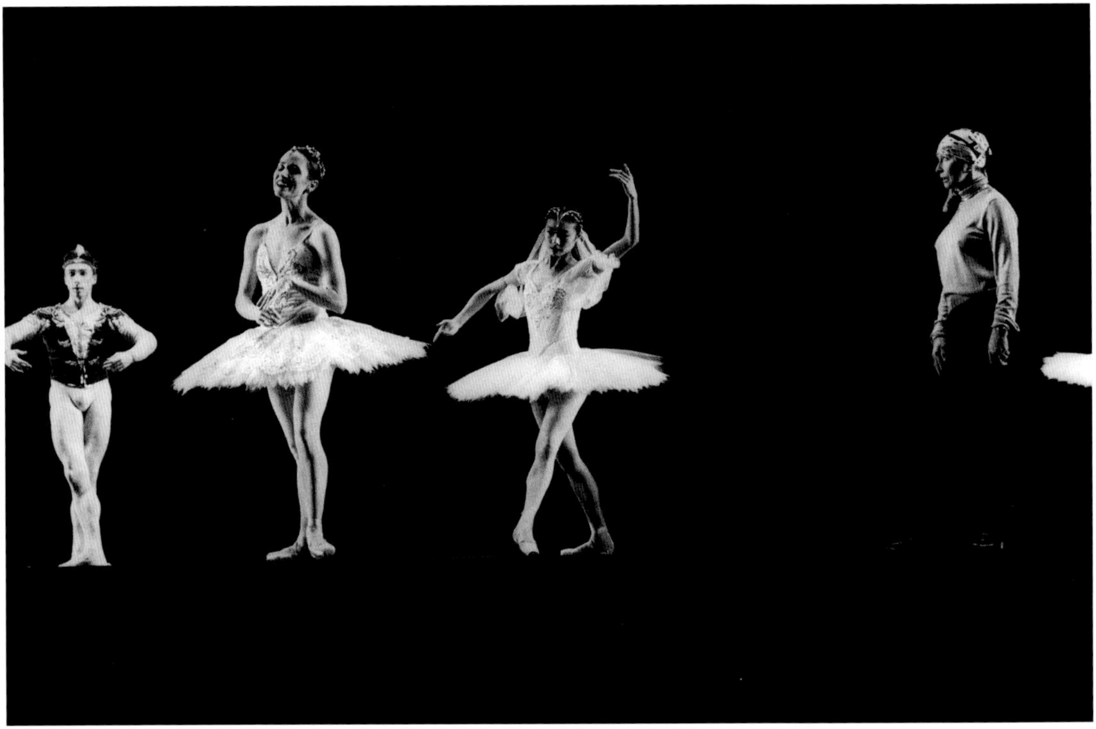

Principal dancers Roman Rykine, Tina, and Yuan Yuan Tan, with the great Russian dancer and choreographer Natalia Makarova, who is setting her rendition of *The Kingdom of the Shades* from *La Bayadère*. As a child, Tina had imagined herself having a baby and continuing to dance, because Makarova had done so in the 1970s. (2000)

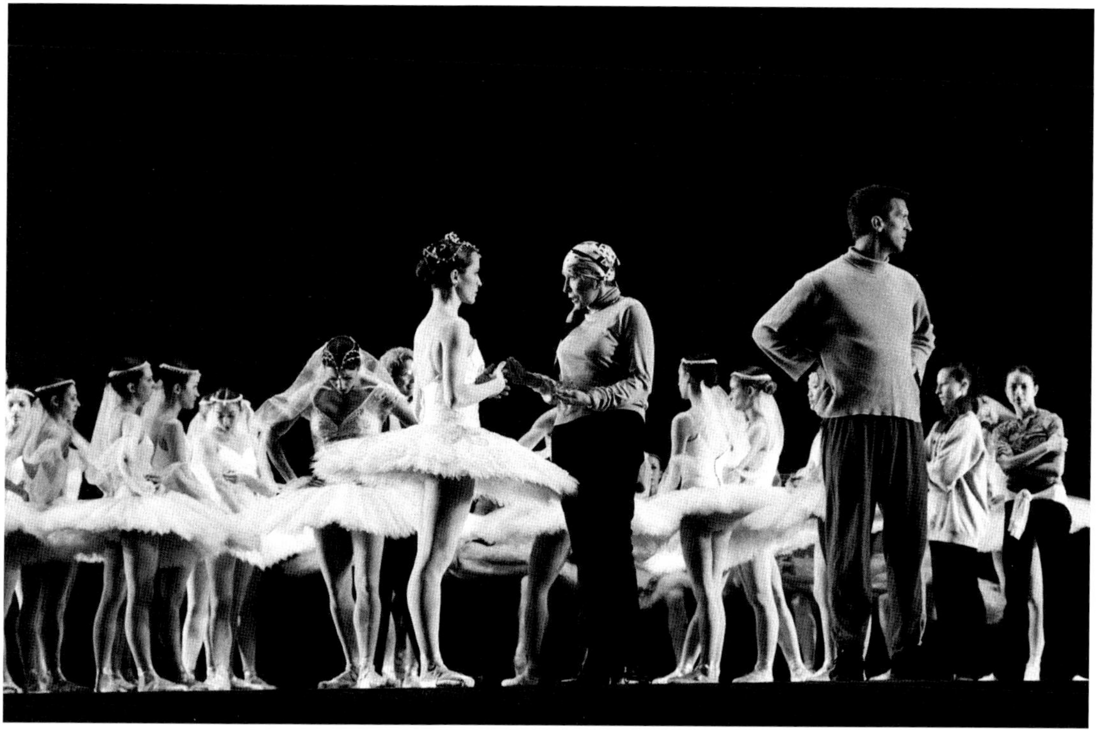

Makarova gives Tina notes during a full cast rehearsal of *The Kingdom of the Shades*. Lorena Feijoo is to the left of Tina, and Ashley Wheater is to the right of Makarova. (2000)

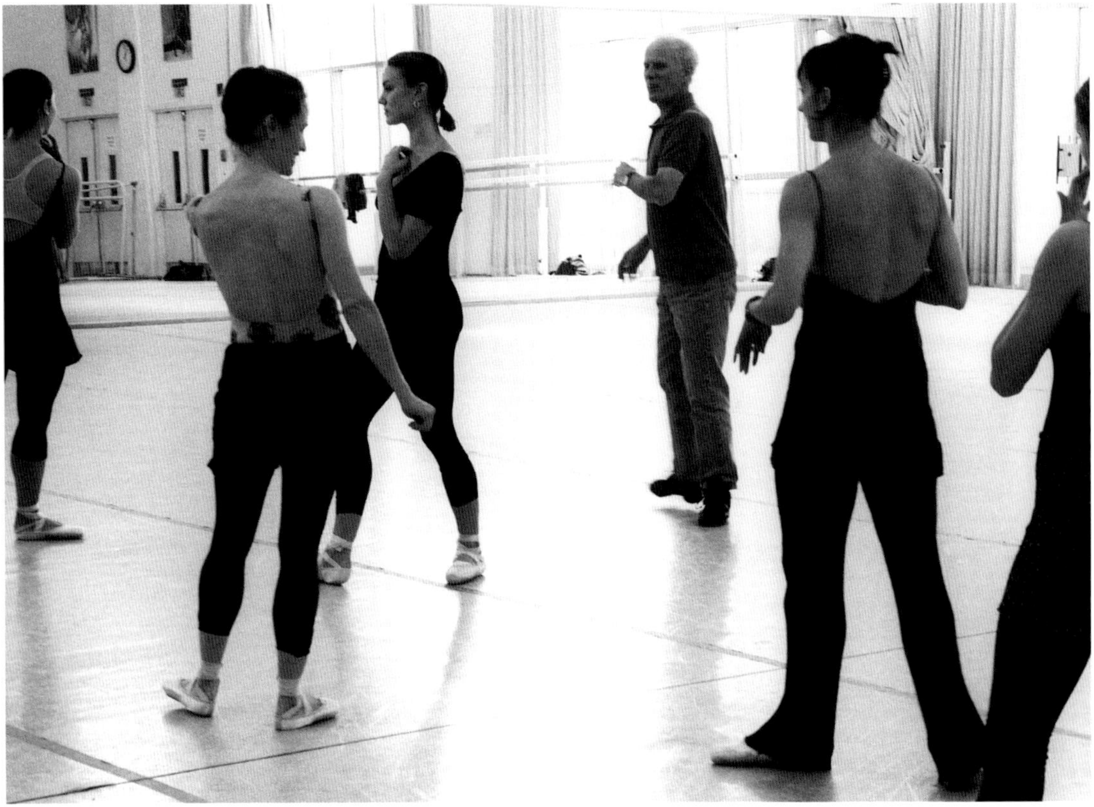

Helgi directs class. Tina (middle, with her back to us) seems to bring out a playful side of him.
Lorena Feijoo is to the right of Helgi. (2000)

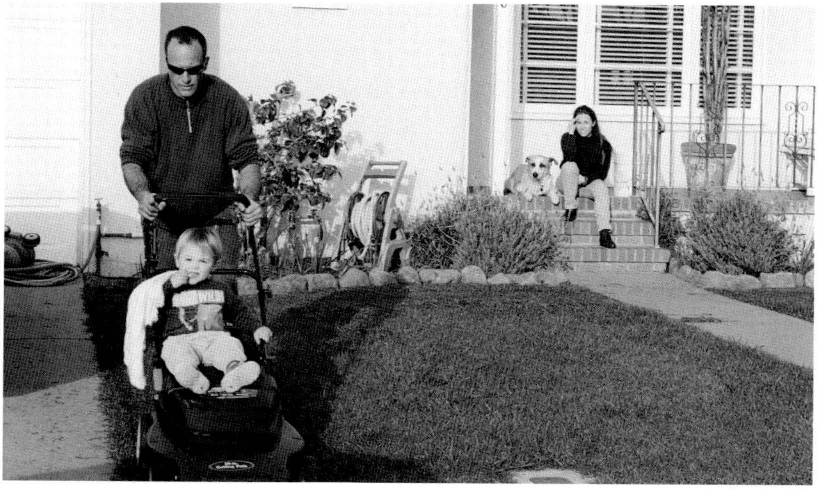

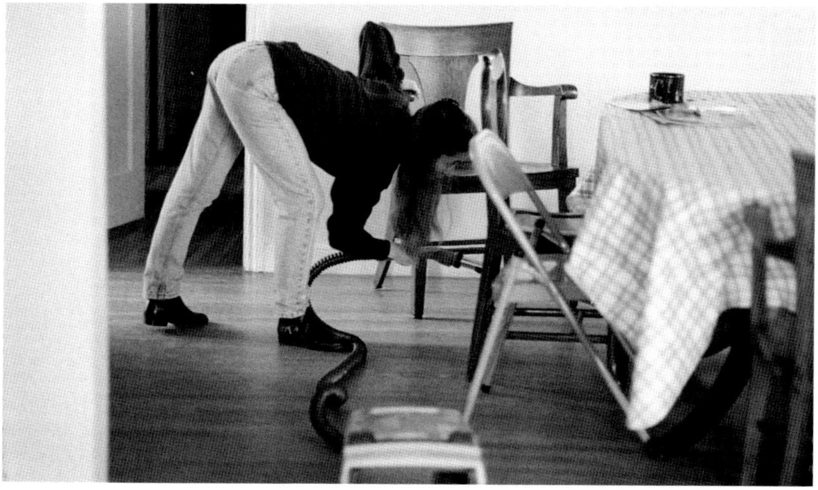

top
Marco, Marinko, and Tina at home. (2002)

bottom
Tina at home vacuuming on Monday, her one day off each week during the dancing season. (2002)

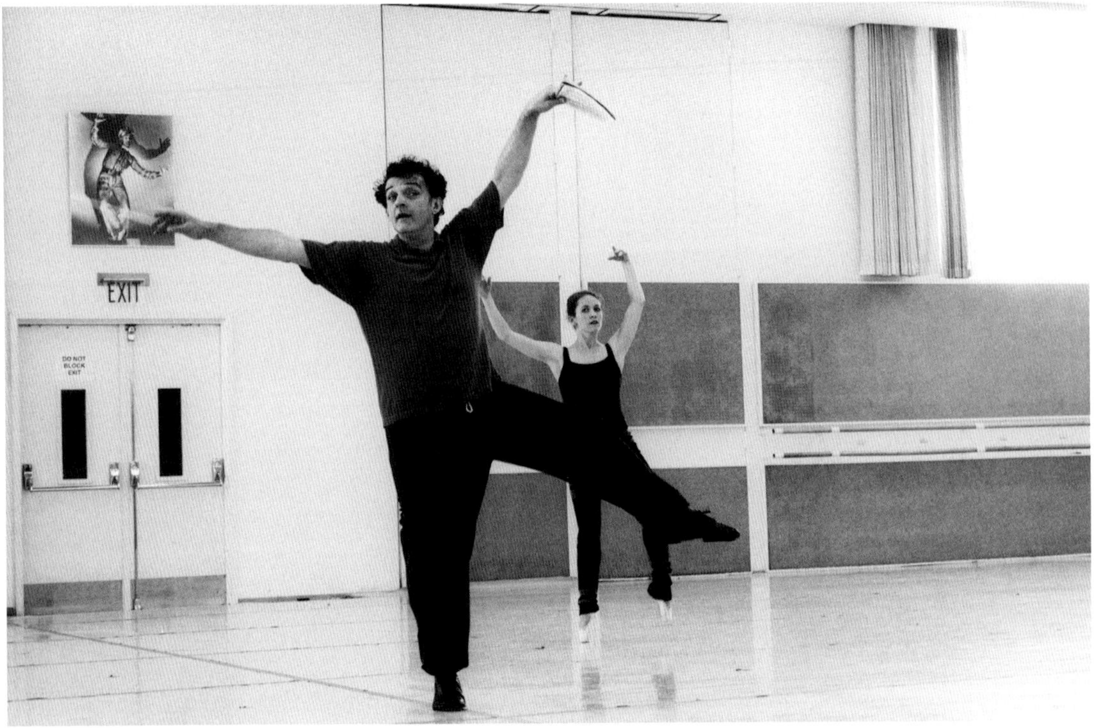

Mark Morris setting his dance *A Garden*, commissioned by San Francisco Ballet, to Tina. (2000)

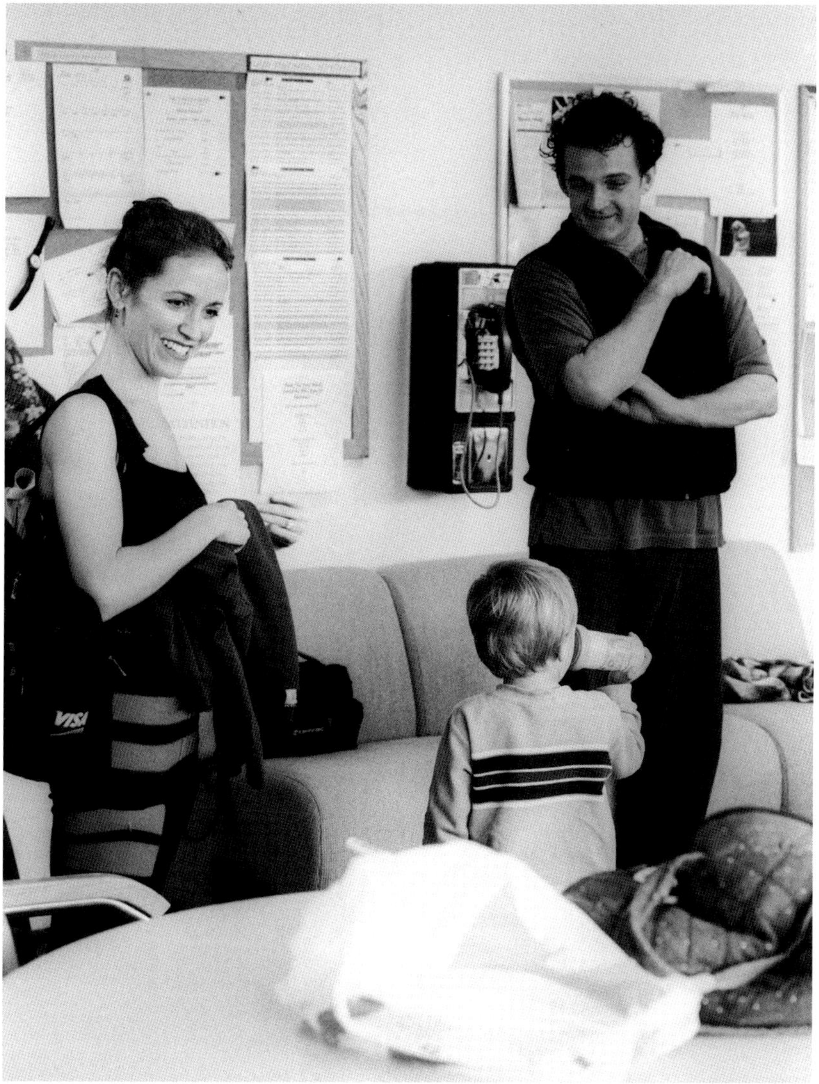

Tina, Marinko, and Mark Morris in the dancers' lounge after rehearsal. (2000)

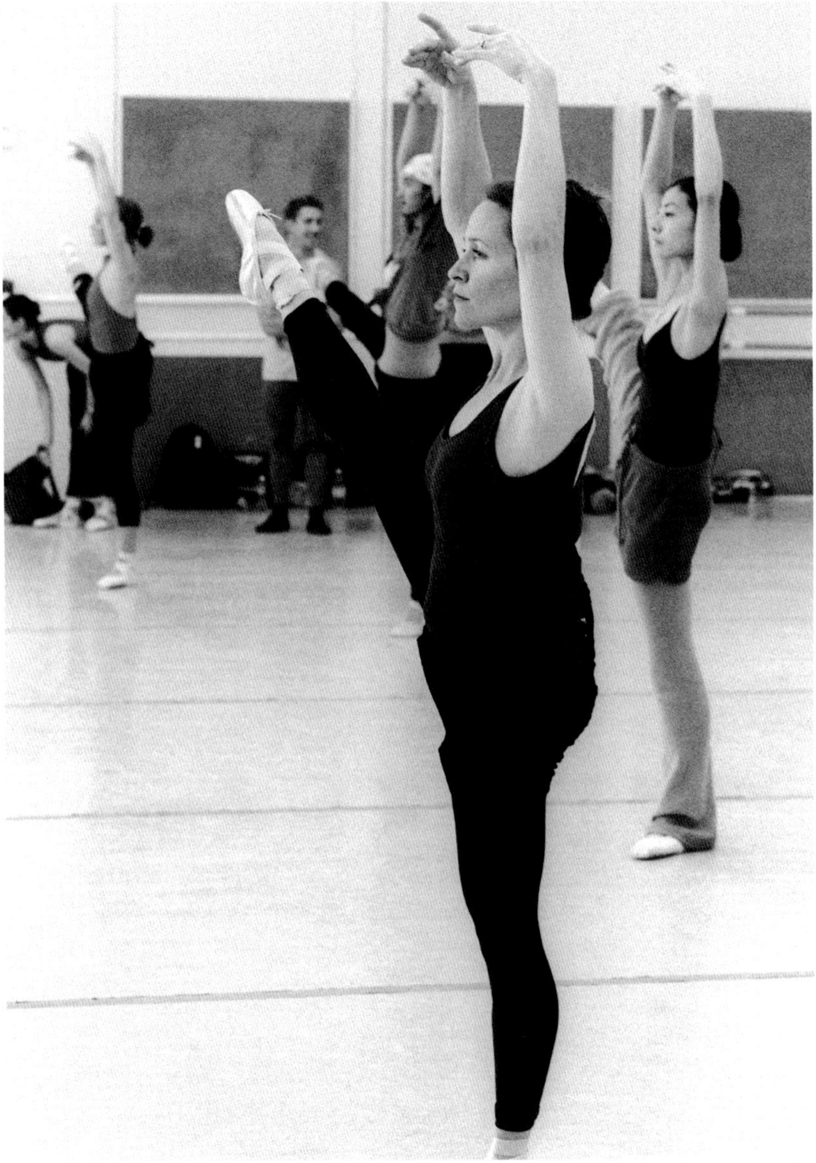

Tina takes class when she is three months and eight months pregnant. (2002 and 2003)

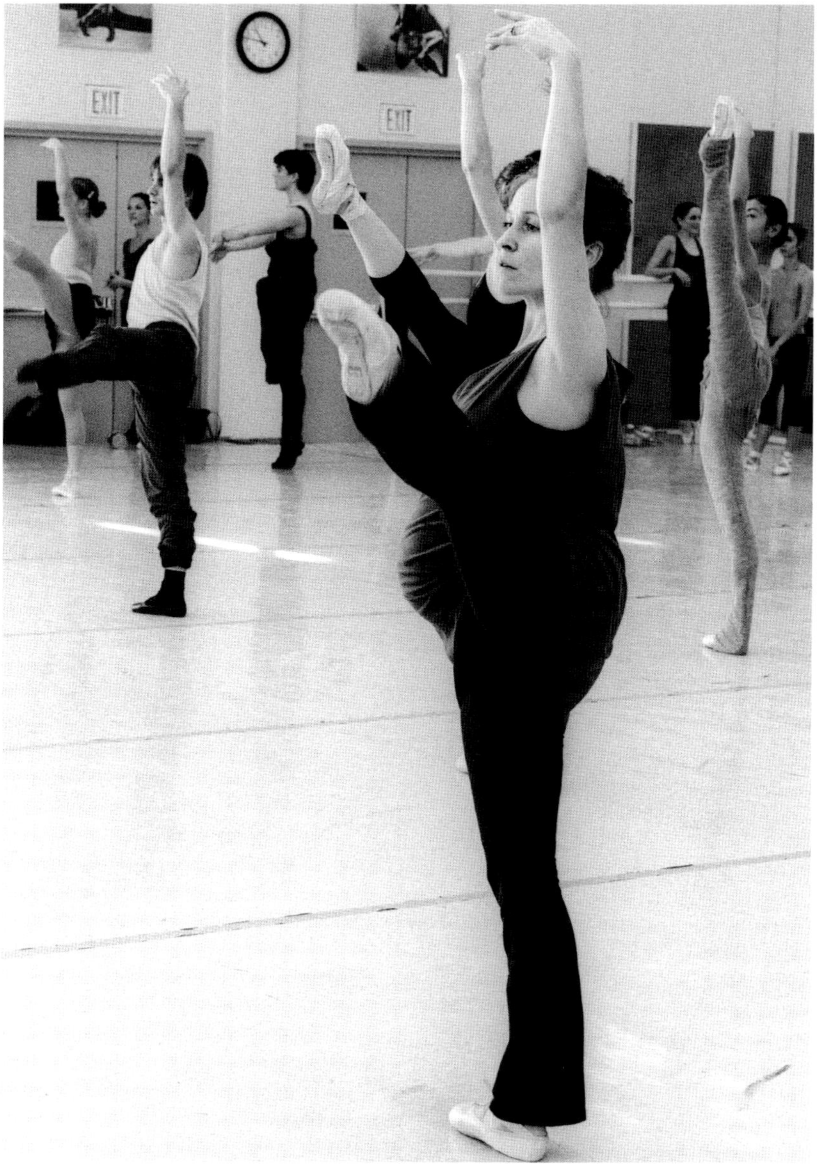
EXIT
EXIT

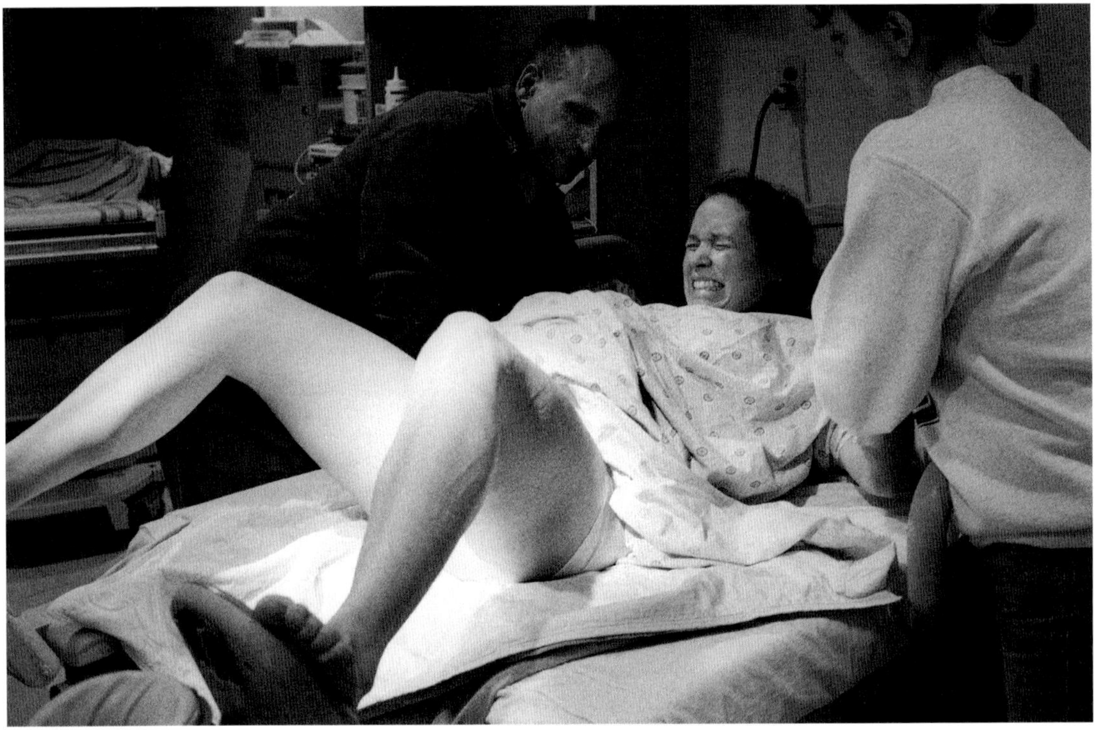

above
Tina gives birth, with her husband, Marco Jerkunica, and her sister, Sherri, at California Pacific Medical Center. (2003)

right
Marco and Tina with Sasha Johan Jerkunica, born February 1, 2003.

overleaf
Sasha has been fed and is napping, so Tina can work out. (2003)

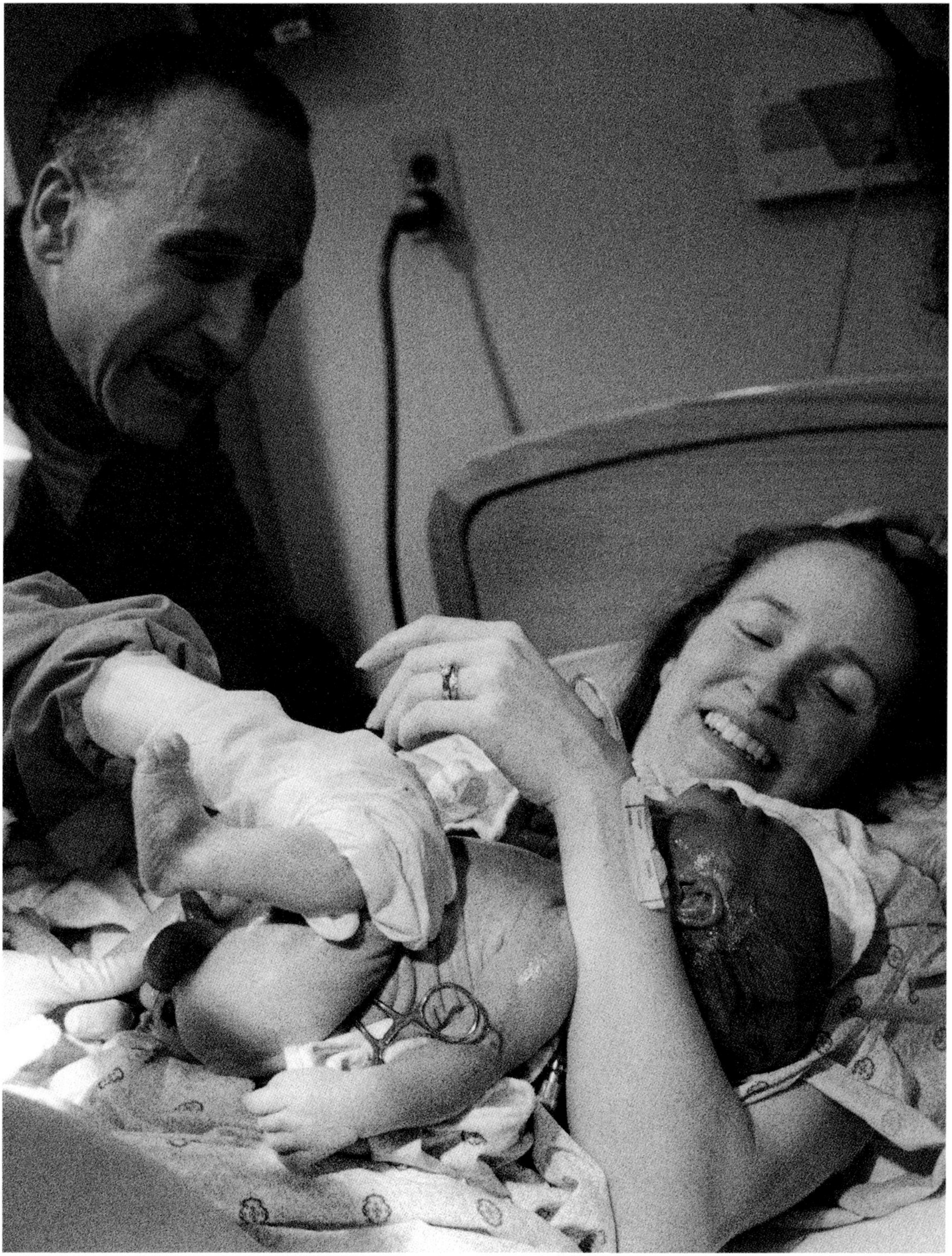

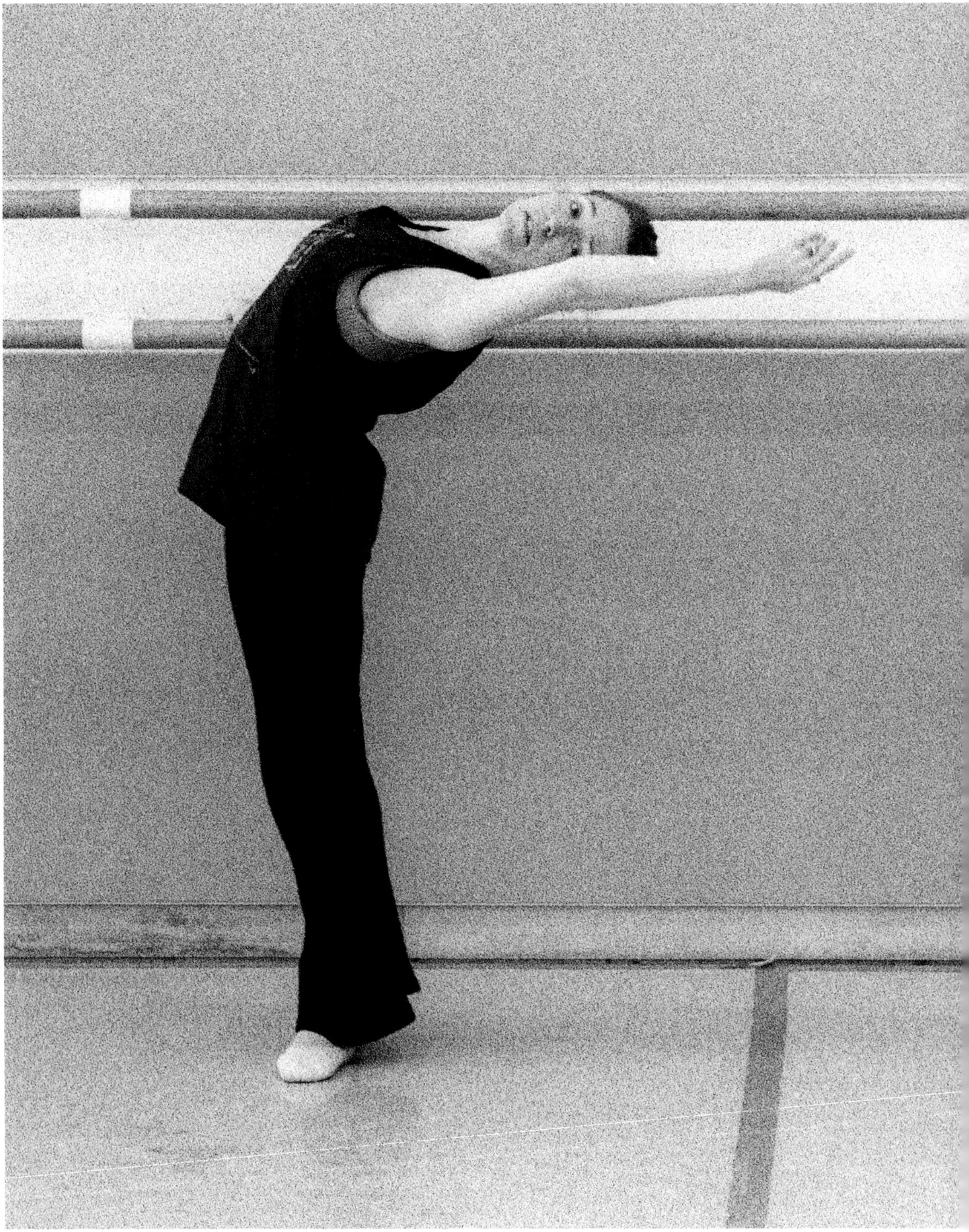

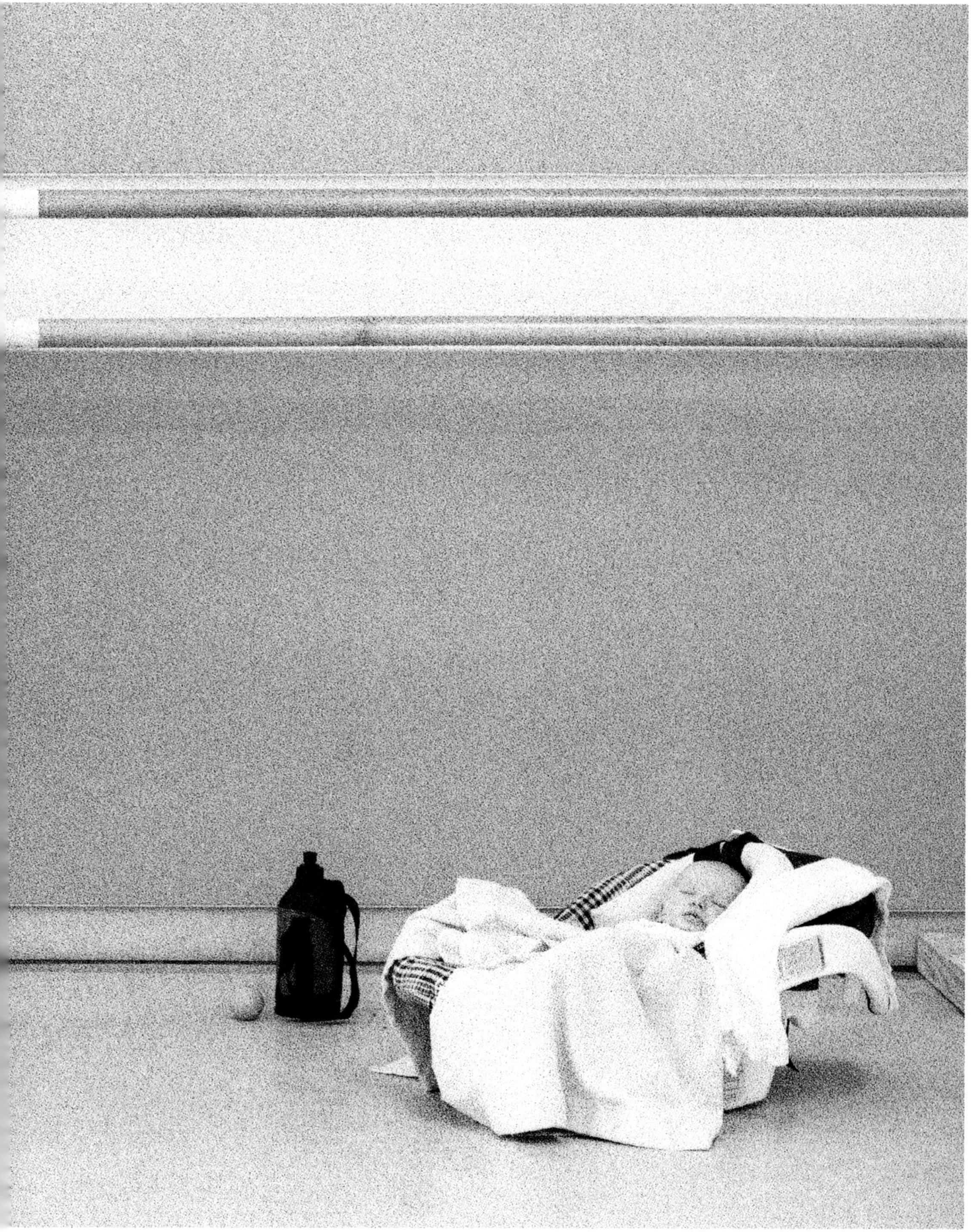

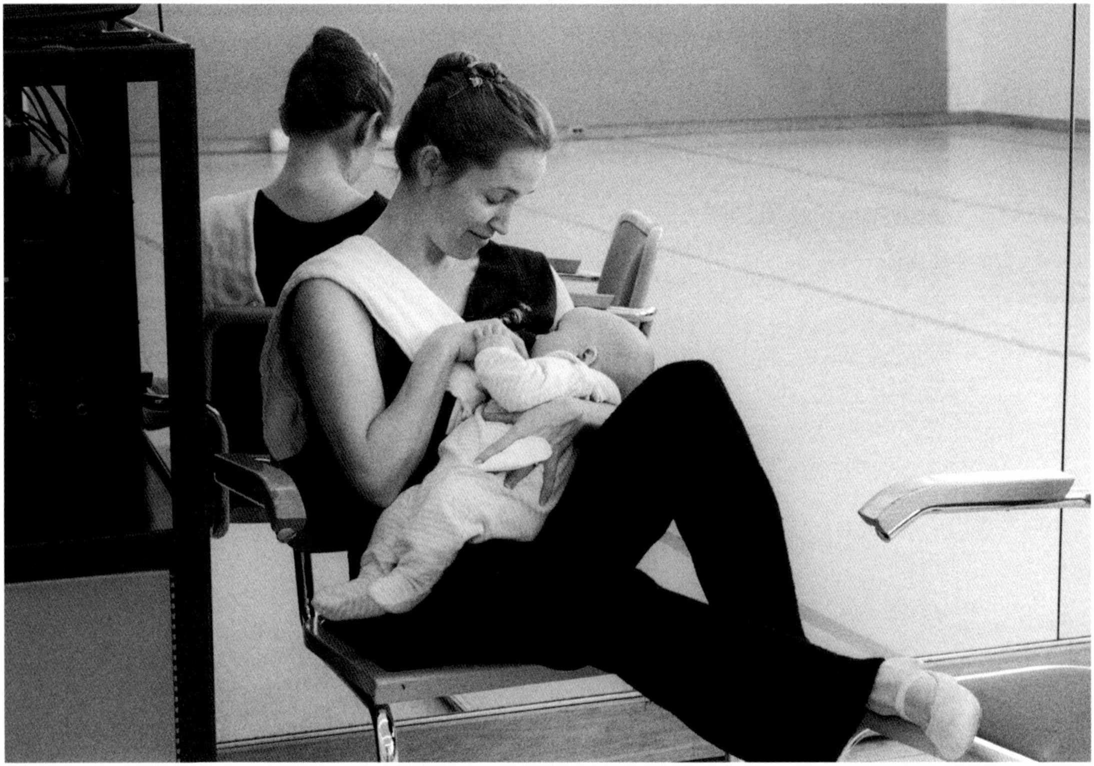

Tina feeds six-week-old Sasha. (2003)

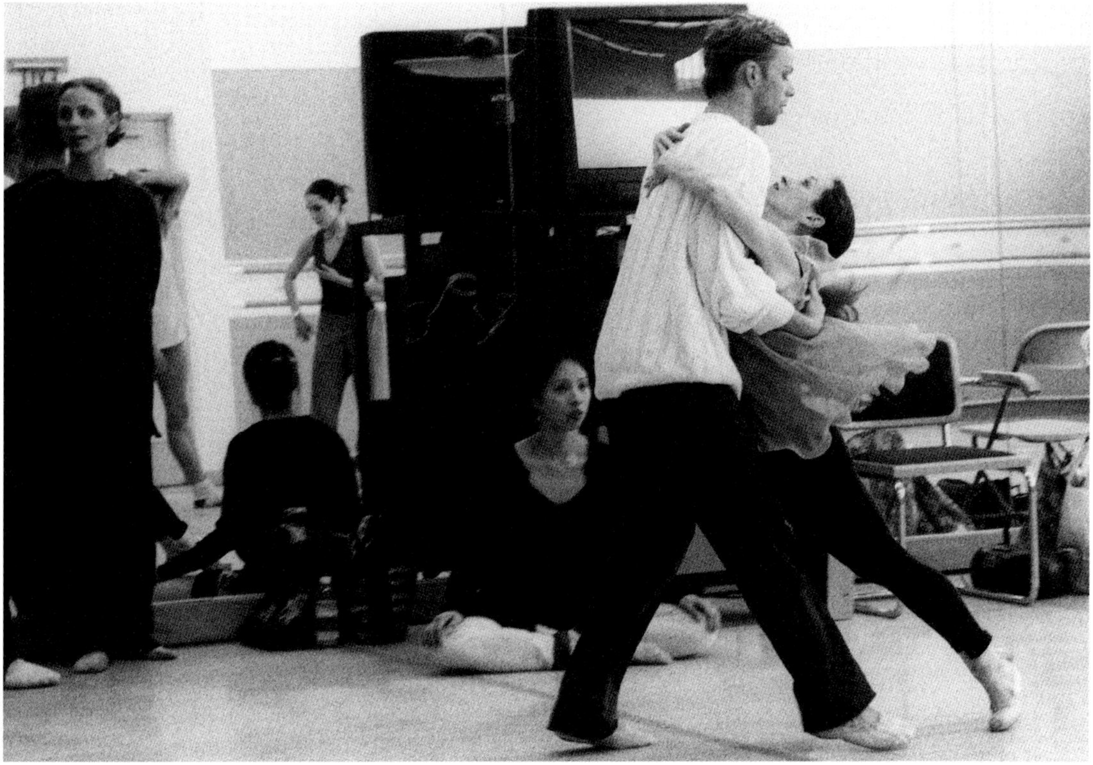

above

Julia Adam (back to the mirror, left) is a dancer at the company who is becoming a choreographer. Here she sets her work *Night* to Tina. From left: Leslie Young, Vadim Solomakha, and Tina. (2000)

overleaf

Tina, Peter Brandenhoff, and Benjamin Pierce (a dancer who also designed these dreamy costumes reminiscent of jellyfish) perform the world premiere of *Night*. (2000)

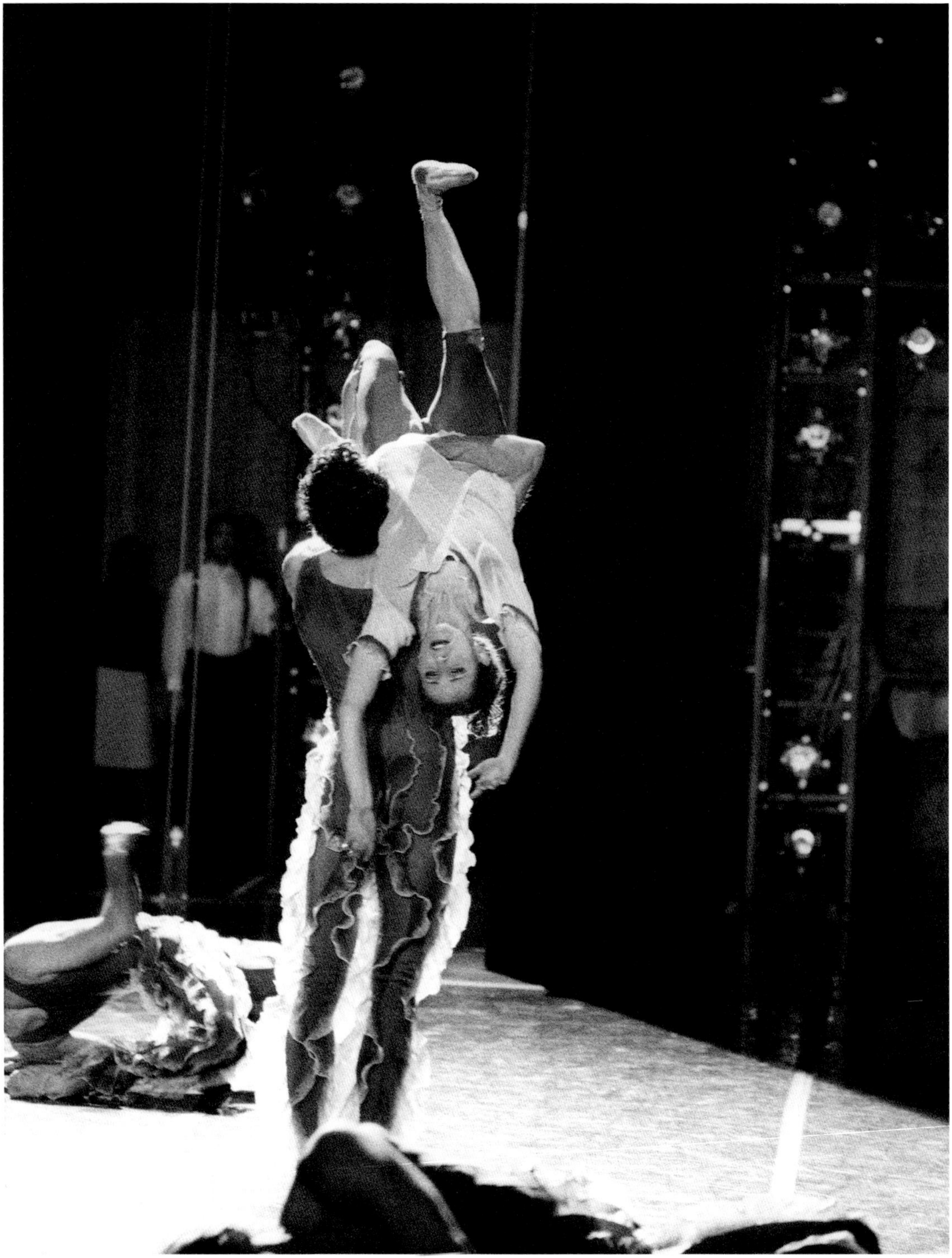

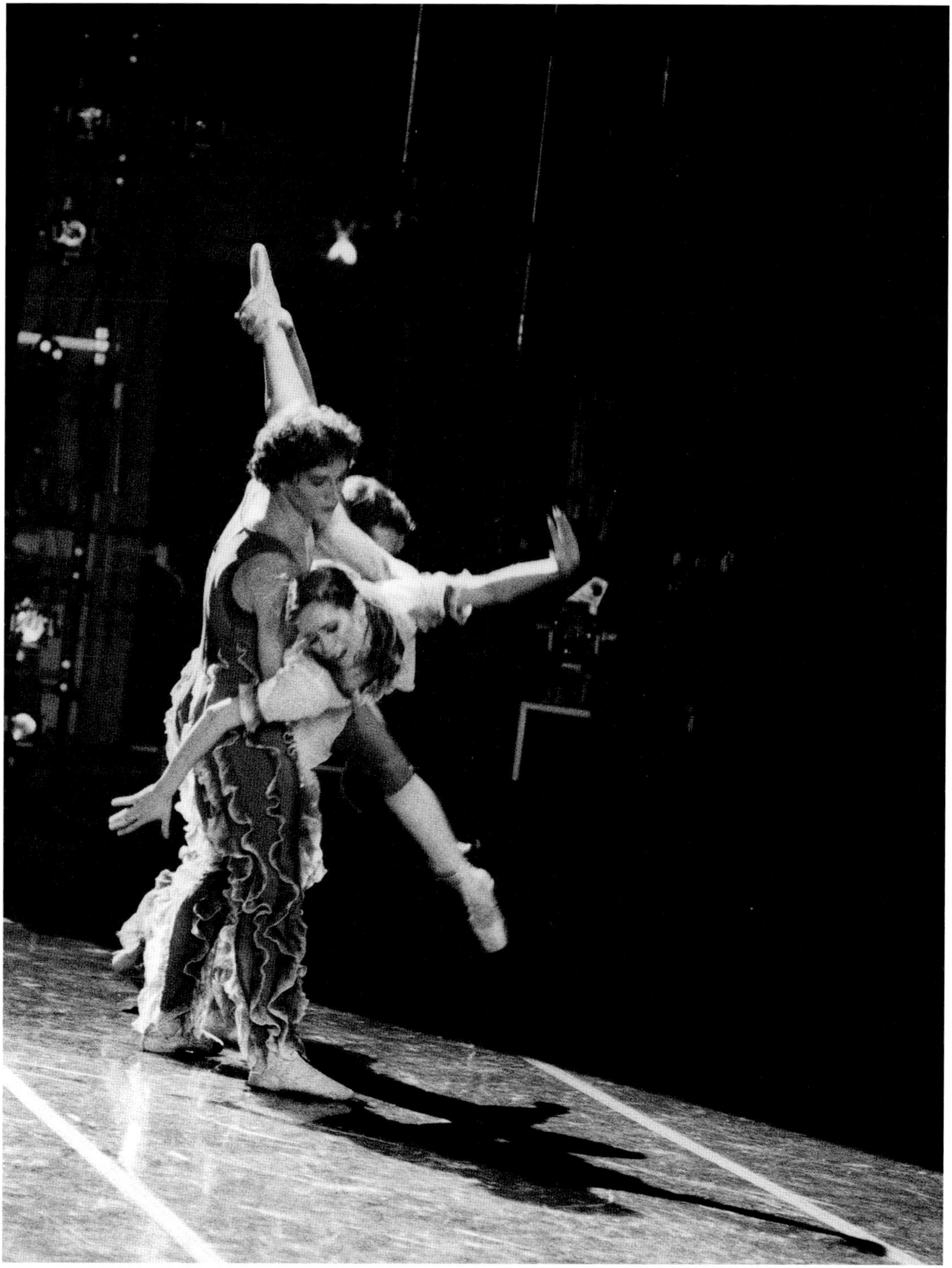

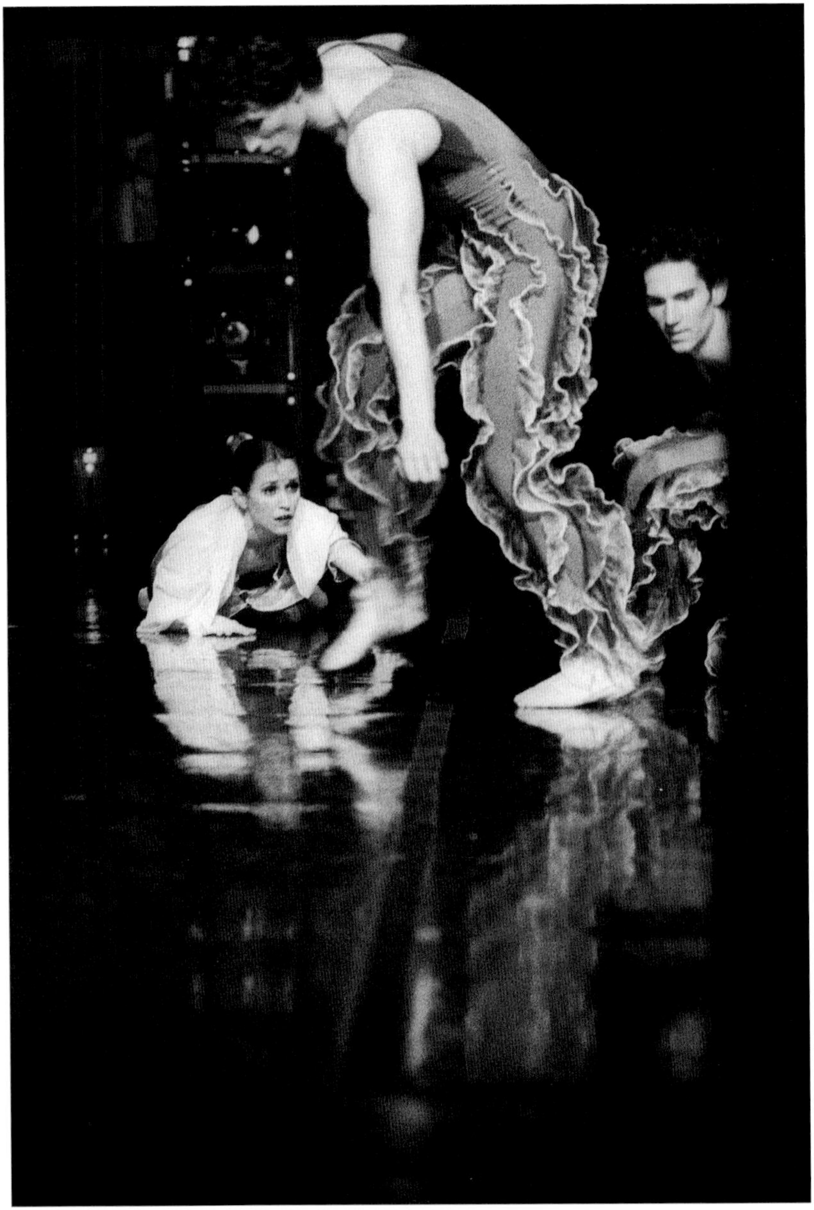

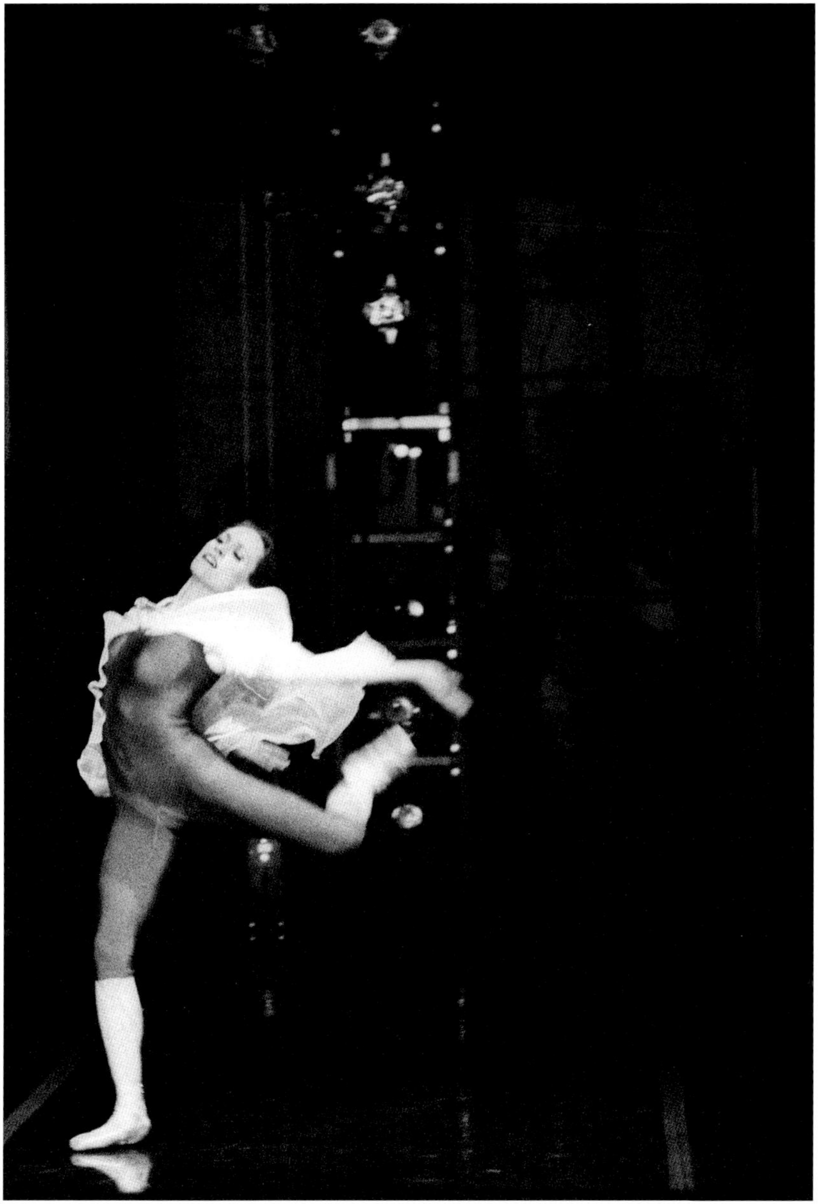

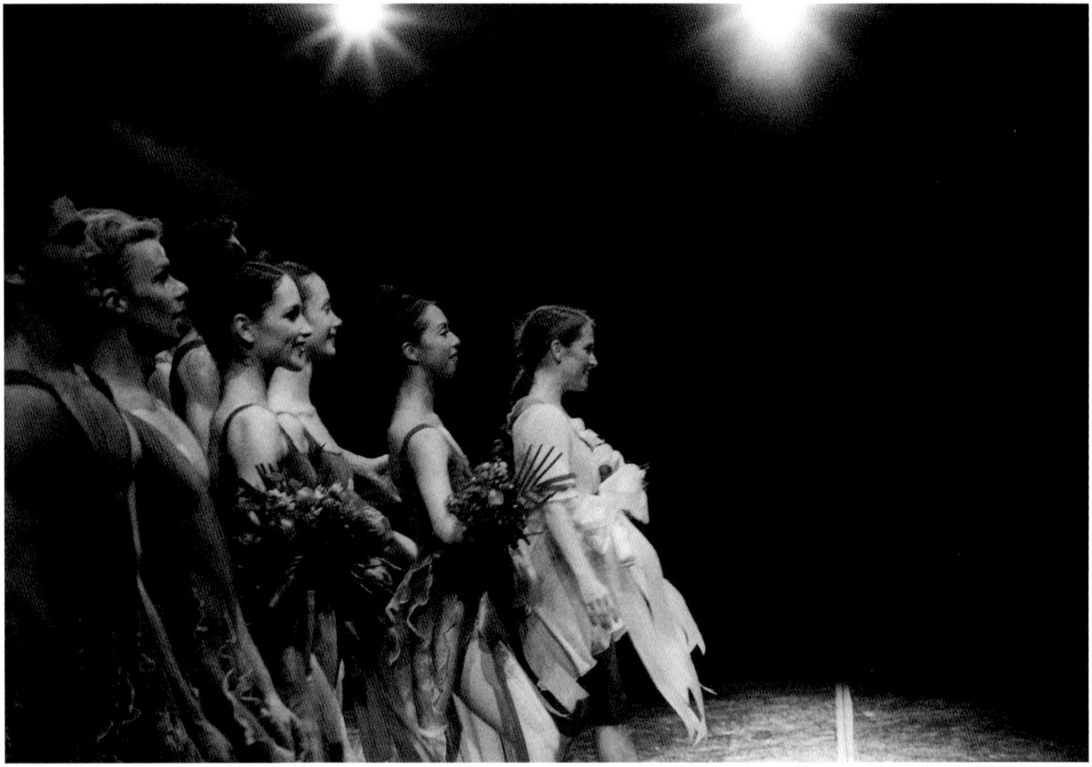

above
Tina and cast of *Night* take a bow. (2000)

right
Tina in a San Francisco Ballet advertisement on the corner of Third and Twenty-Second Streets in San Francisco. The ad appears on buses, bus stops, and banners all over the city, as well as in magazines and newspapers. (2000)

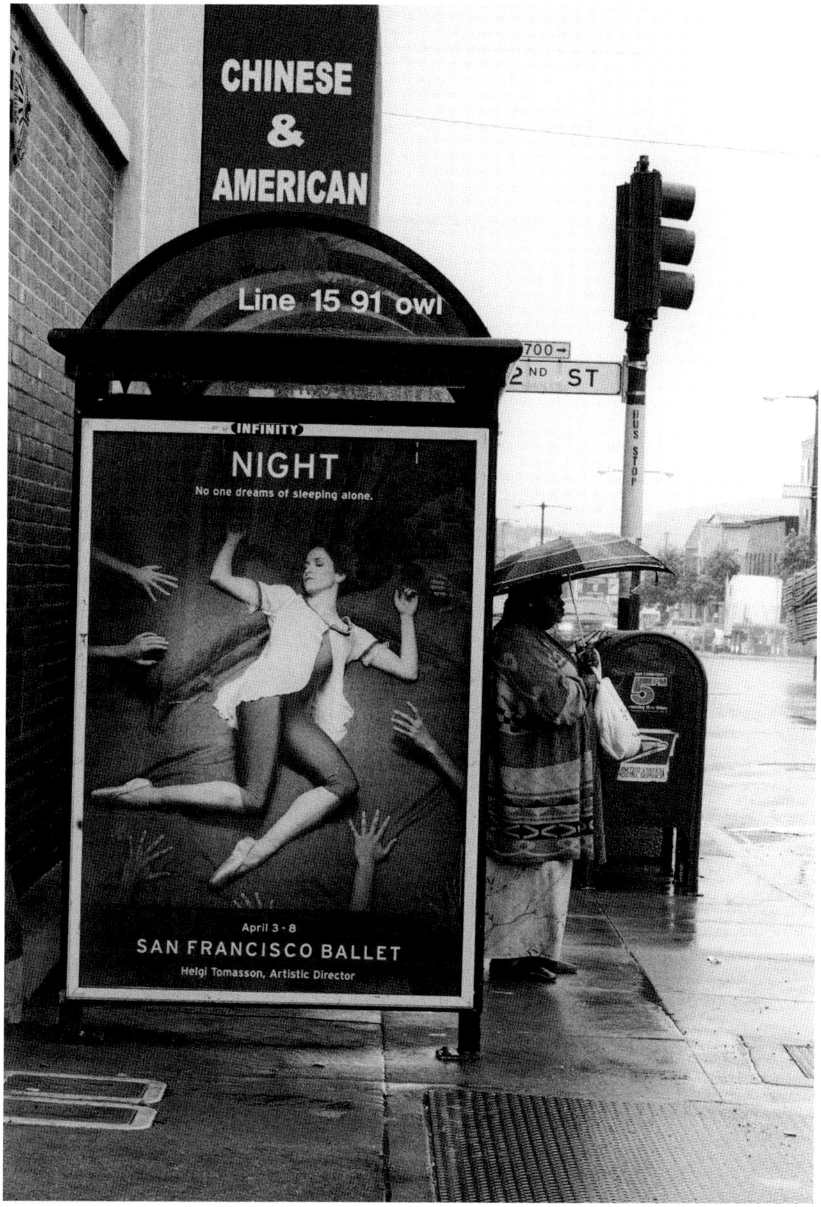
CHINESE
&
AMERICAN
Line 15 91 owl
700→
2ND ST
BUS STOP
INFINITY
NIGHT
No one dreams of sleeping alone.
April 3 - 8
SAN FRANCISCO BALLET
Helgi Tomasson, Artistic Director

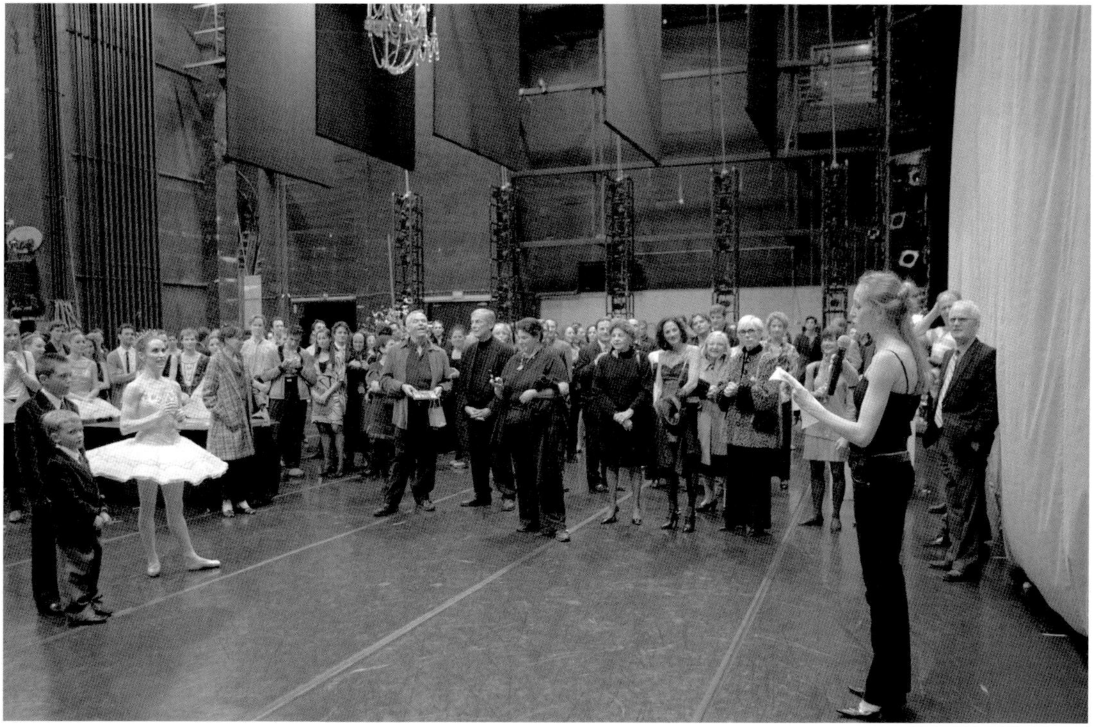

above

The curtain is down and lights are up on the entire cast, along with ballet staff and friends, backstage at the War Memorial Opera House. Sasha, Marinko, and Tina listen to Katita's farewell toast as Helgi (to Katita's right) watches with amusement. (2009)

left

Onstage after Tina's farewell performance of four pas de deux with four different partners from four ballets that she chose, her arms are open for Katita and Kristin and theirs for her. (2009)

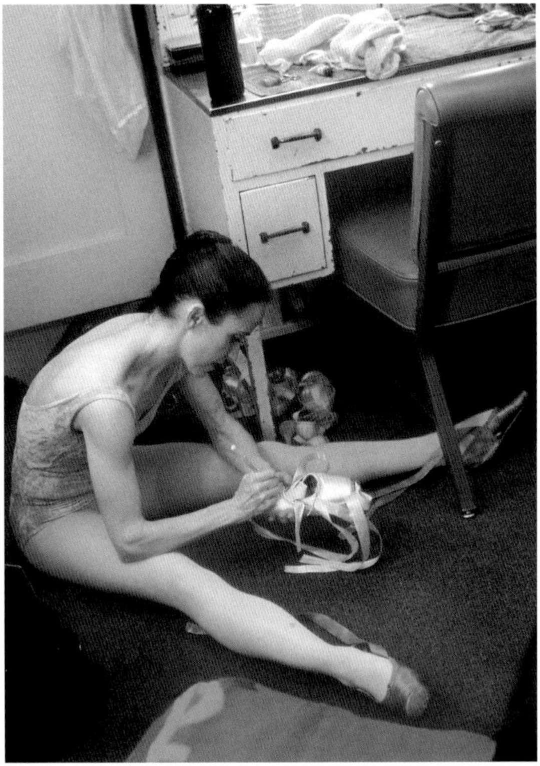

Tina signs slippers she has danced in to be sold as souvenirs at the San Francisco Ballet Company Shop. (2009)

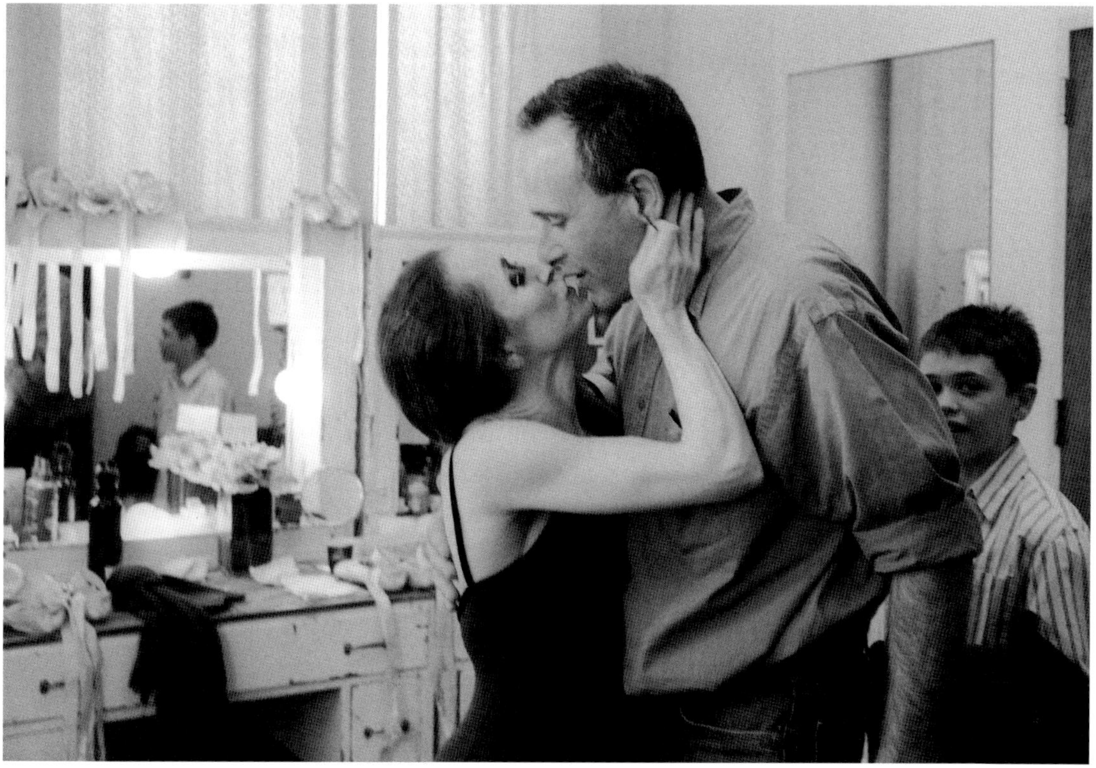

In her dressing room after her farewell performance, Tina kisses Marco as their son Marinko looks on. (2009)

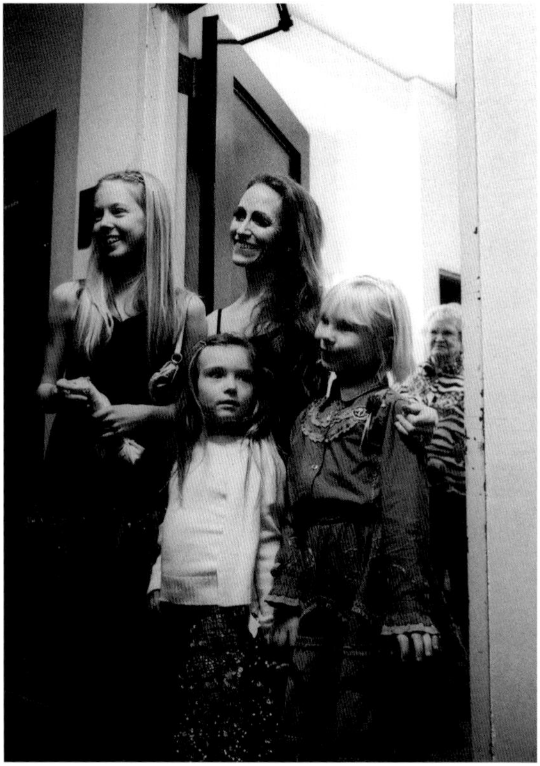

above

Tina poses for a picture with fans after her farewell performance. Tina's mother, Shirley Jane LeBlanc, watches from inside the dressing room. (2009)

right

The last time Tina will stand—five feet one in her leotard—at the stage door of the San Francisco Ballet. Notice the handle is above her head. (2009)

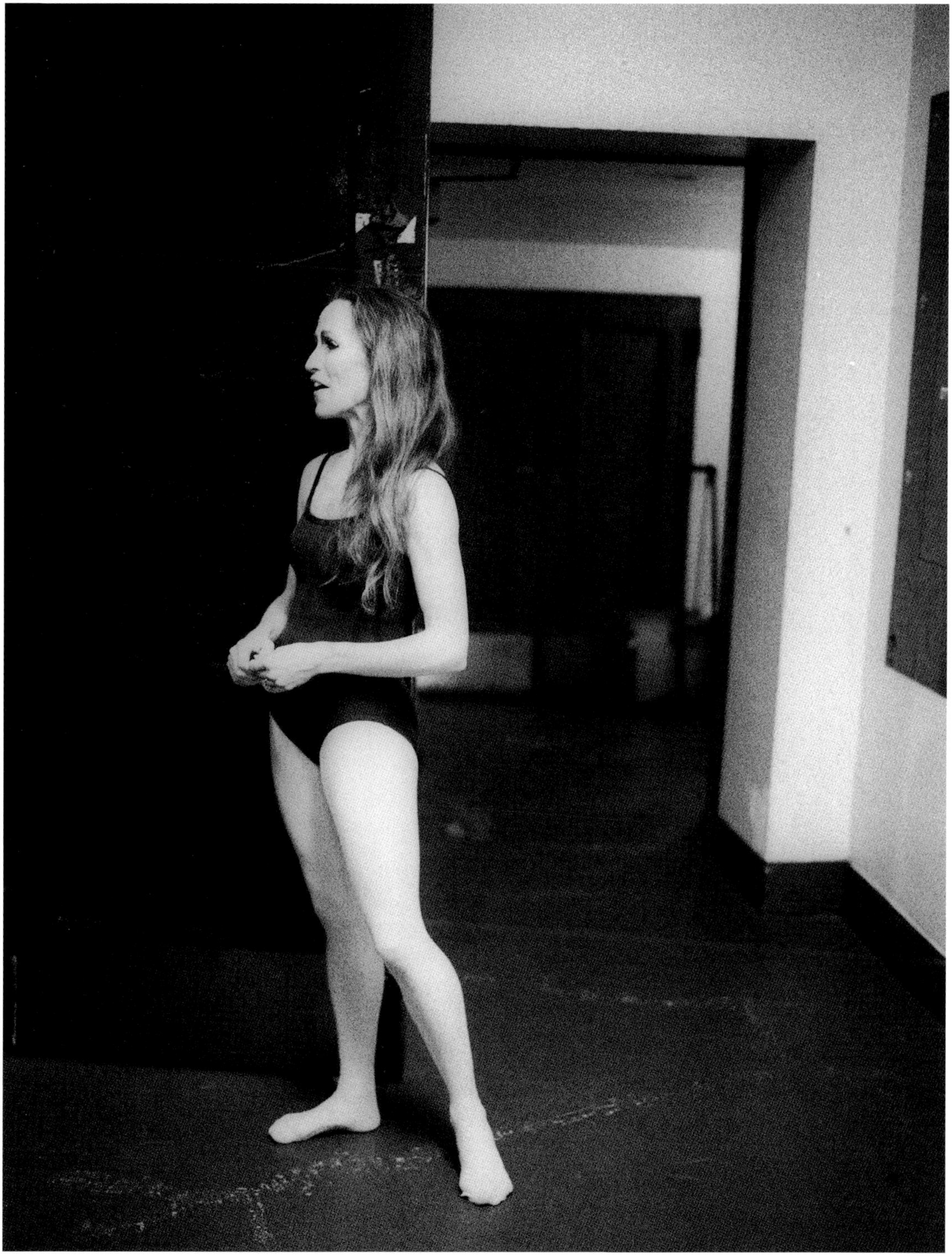

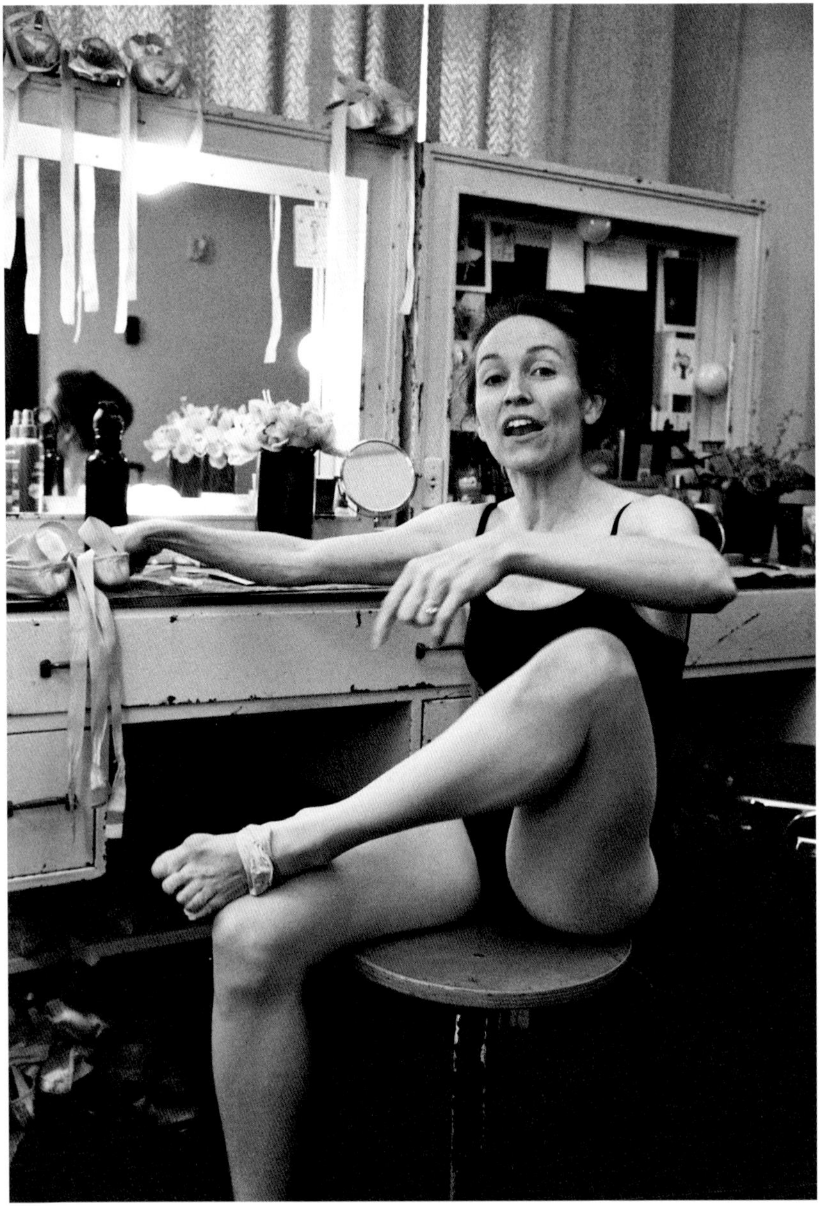

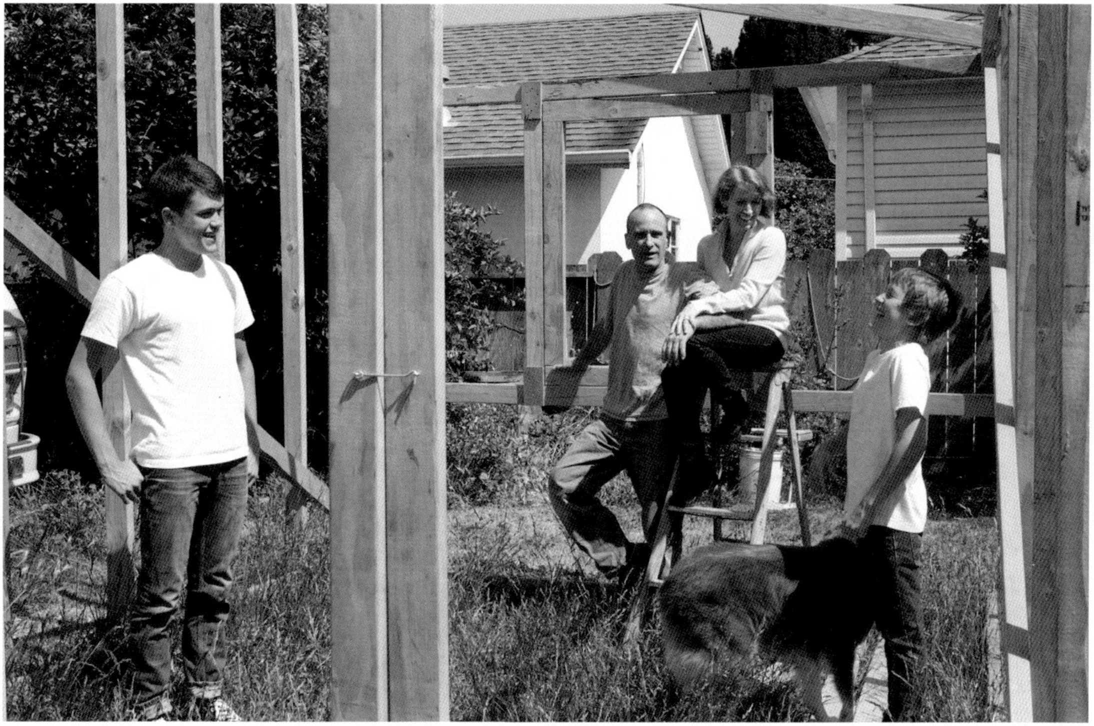

above

Tina at home with her family: Marinko, Marco, Tina, and Sasha (telling a joke) are standing in a greenhouse they are building. Work isn't going as fast as it might because Marco, having been out of work for three years, was recently asked by his old partner to restart their contracting business. (San Mateo, 2014)

left

Tina in the dressing room, having taken off her pointe shoes after her last dance for San Francisco Ballet. (2009)

KATITA WALDO

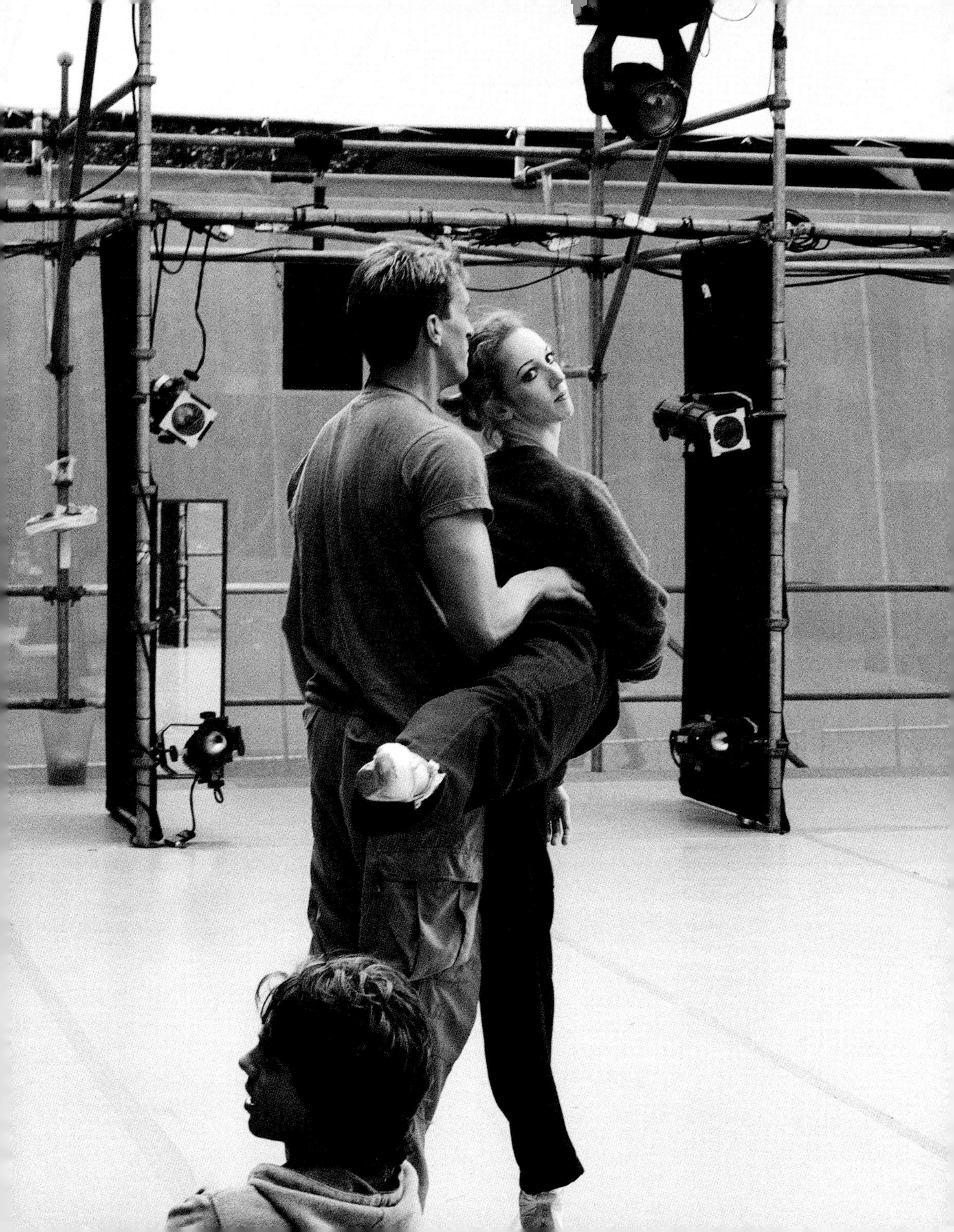

APR 9, 1968	Born Kathryn Cristine Waldo Grey in Madrid, Spain
1973	Studies at Escuela de Danza Classica under Artistic Director Alain Baldini
1979	Moves to Ithaca, New York, and studies at Ithaca Ballet under Artistic Director Alice Reid
1981	Enrolls in University of North Carolina School of the Arts in Winston-Salem, North Carolina
1983	Meets Marshall Crutcher
1984	Studies at Washington Ballet under Michael Steele
1986	Moves to San Francisco; studies at San Francisco Ballet under Larissa Sklyanskaya, Henry Berg, and Anatole Vilzak (among others)
1987	Named apprentice at SFB under Artistic Director Helgi Tomasson
1988	Joins SFB as a member of the corps de ballet under Artistic Director Helgi Tomasson
1989	Marries Marshall Crutcher
1990	Promoted to soloist at SFB under Artistic Director Helgi Tomasson
1994	Promoted to principal dancer at SFB under Artistic Director Helgi Tomasson
AUG 16, 1999	Gives birth to James Tiberius Crutcher
2001-02 SEASON	Receives Isadora Duncan Dance Award
2004	Serves as ballet master and choreographer's assistant for Christopher Wheeldon at Bolshoi Ballet, Moscow, Russia
2006-2007	Serves as ballet master and choreographer's assistant for Yuri Possokhov at Bolshoi Ballet, Moscow, Russia
2010	Retires from SFB as a dancer and becomes a ballet master under Artistic Director Helgi Tomasson
2013	Comes out of retirement to perform the Stepmother in Christopher Wheeldon's *Cinderella*

KATITA WALDO | APRIL 2002

I grew up in a very happy family. It was just me and my parents, which I grew to love. I wanted a brother for a long time, until I realized I'd have to share my parents with him. My earliest memories are of dancing. I used to put *Swan Lake* on and dance the whole thing—in my crib, my mom says. My parents played classical music all the time. My dad was a jazz lover—Louis Armstrong, Duke Ellington, Sidney Bechet. He liked singers like Billie Holiday. My mom was in the film business in Spain. She was the first woman to graduate from a Spanish film school. They were bohemian free spirits.

My parents took me to a production of *Swan Lake* when I was five, and I still have this image of the tutus, the blue lights, and me dancing down the street afterward. Then they enrolled me in dance class. I didn't like it at all. I wanted to *dance*. I didn't want to do those stupid exercises. That was not my idea of a good time. I said, "Mom, I want to stop." She said, "That's fine, but I paid for a year. Just finish the year." At the end of the year they did an evaluation performance, and that was it. I loved performing. My father has a picture of me. I have little, dirty, wrinkly knees. I won first place.

I always loved it, but it didn't hit me that this was what I'd do until I came to the States when I was eleven. When I was a kid I was considered super, super gifted. I was very competitive. In Spain I was the first one to get to the older level, and the other girls gave me grief about that. I was better than everyone my age. I could tell it would be easy for me. In Spain there weren't that many girls who were going to be professional. But here, these girls were good. This was in Ithaca, New York; I was lucky because I got to dance with the Ithaca Ballet. The training was exceptional. They trained you to be professional.

I was lucky because boys wouldn't touch me with a ten-foot pole. Thank God. I looked like Opie's younger sister, as my husband tells me. I weighed sixty-nine pounds. I was four feet, nine inches tall. I had big, huge glasses. I was not attractive. I was a geek. But there was always something about me that was sexual. The kids my own age didn't like me, but I disturbed the teachers. It was weird. I felt I was exciting men at eleven. But at the same time I was so insecure because the guys I really wanted were like, "Ewww." So it was this twisted thing: "I know what you want. I have it. But you don't see it." The only time I felt powerful and complete, so that I could use my sexuality, and it worked, and it was good, was when I danced.

From eleven to twelve I went to public school. Then it became apparent that, dancewise, I could probably go somewhere better. It also became obvious to my parents that I was so demoralized in public school that I just couldn't go anymore. I auditioned for the University of North Carolina School of the Arts. They accepted me at thirteen. My parents didn't want me to go. They thought I was a year too young, but I was going to have a nervous breakdown if I continued on the way I was. So off I went to boarding school in Winston-Salem, North Carolina.

My first year I started to develop tendinitis in my hips. The second year it got really bad, and I pulled out of the school. I was a scholarship student. I won an award that paid for therapy in New York. In retrospect I think I was in crisis because dance had always been so easy for me. I felt guilty if I didn't do it. Then I wasn't sure I wanted to. But while I was out for eight months, I was saying, "This is my identity. What will happen if I can't do it?" I was fifteen.

I went back to school and met Marshall. He was my first and only lover. It's not like there hasn't been groping here and there in these eighteen years, but Marshall and I got serious when I was very young, and I've never been with anyone else. And that's fine.

I get crushes on my partners constantly. But I've never met a soul mate. My husband is my soul mate. Plus, I think that he's gorgeous. Dancing is fun because it's perfection. You touch the toe, you lift the toe, you go for it. Sometimes dancing is better than sex. Drives Marshall crazy because I'll come home and say, "I'm tired. I've had sex all day. It's enough." Sometimes ballet is more romantic than it is sexual. Because you know each other so well, you can do things with these people that would make most people say, "Oh, my God!" You'd have to go really far to overstep the boundaries.

I went to a baby shower six years before James was born—I was twenty-six, twenty-seven, and I woke up the next morning, and I wanted a baby. Somebody turned the switch. I waited and waited because of my tentative position here. Financially we were afraid. People here had children, but they all left. Then Kristin and Tina got pregnant. Tina was here, so I watched her very carefully to see how things went for her. More importantly, I wanted to see how her career went when she came back.

We started trying one year. It didn't work, so we stopped. We waited till the following year, and it took. I was in Russia, and I took a test, and I was pregnant. I wasn't going to tell anyone, but we were in Russia, and everyone was drinking. I wouldn't. Everyone knows me, so they wanted to know what was going on. I can't keep my mouth shut, so I told everyone.

Helgi was wonderful. His main concern was that I was making the right life decision. Dancing, *shmancing*—this was a huge deal! I danced fully through my fourth month. I did Desdemona in *Othello*. Thanks to Helgi, I was able to use my sick days cleverly. I came back and did pliés a week after James was born. I learned the mother in *Giselle*, a character part. But of course, now I'll never get out of it. But it's OK because it always reminds me of James. I went on tour and did the mother when James was eight weeks old. I managed to stay paid through the season.

KATITA WALDO | SEPTEMBER 2002

[Getting back into physical shape after I had James] was very easy. The hardest thing was getting my back in order. I kept waiting to have pain in my feet, but it never happened—probably because of the estrogen and the hormones and all of that stuff. I breast-fed for nine months. Actually, the thing that I had the hardest time with was keeping weight on. I went back to my regular schedule, and I was dancing really hard. I heard through the grapevine that Helgi was worried because I was too skinny. I think it was the estrogen that kept me from gaining muscle bulk. I stayed soft, which made me look even skinnier.

It was particularly hard when James was an infant because he was so helpless. Once they start developing a decisive personality, they can guide you as to who they like and who they don't, what works for them, what doesn't. But when they're teensy little babies—it was hard for me because he had to go into day care at about ten weeks, which was agony. I didn't want to do that. I wanted to be with him more. That was the hardest part. I had to get back into shape so I could get my paycheck, and Marshall had to work so we could feed the child. We had a really bad first day-care situation. It was horrible. That was one of the most sickening feelings of my life. It worked out—we found him a nanny that he really liked, and then she hooked us up with a little home day care that was a block from where we lived. That was heaven. He went there for a year and loved it. There were only five kids in the program, all about his age. He thrived—happy, happy little boy.

We committed ourselves to having full day care only four days a week. So for Friday, Saturday, or Sunday we're not covered. And when I'm not working so much, or Marshall isn't, it's fine, but when his work gets crazy—and last year was insanely crazy—it gets really bad. James wasn't old enough to learn to be quiet. He was an attentionmonger. He still is. Now he's able to play by himself a little more, but back then you couldn't do anything—he needed attention 24-7. That was exhausting. But James is older now. We do want to spend time with him. We try to be hands-on parents. We don't plop him down in front of the TV.

I get very down, and when I get depressed, I get distant, and that is hard for [Marshall and James]. Things go badly—I can be depressed—but fundamentally, I am always fine. The only time that ever shakes me is when James is acting up and seemingly unhappy. I don't mind his temper, if he is acting out because he's disturbed. Making the transition from day care to preschool, he's been acting out. He's not the charming little boy that I know. My son having emotional issues is the only thing that will get to me. Emotional issues in other people are fine.

I try to tell him it's OK. I try to get him to talk to me, a lot of holding. He needs you to let him be angry while you hold him, which is difficult. I try to figure out when he needs me to hold him while he tells me he hates me and when it's OK for me to say, "You cannot talk to me that way; you're staying in your room by yourself right now." I know he needs boundaries, I know he needs parameters. We try so hard. There are rules in our house, and he has to stick with them. Trying to enforce those rules at a time when he's discombobulated is difficult, but we're trying to do it all in a good way.

I don't know how much longer I'm going to be dancing, and I don't know how much he'll remember from this time in his life. This may be some vague memory from when he was tiny, instead of the reality of his life. I have ideas for things I'd like to do. I think I have ideas for things I'd be good at. But I don't know that my director agrees with me. I don't know that we see eye to eye. It would be difficult for me to work here if he didn't see me as someone who could foster his vision. He's a very interesting man. He's likely to give people chances and do things with people that are unexpected, so I don't know.

As dancers, we negotiate our yearly salary, and that's what we get paid, whether we dance, don't dance, dance well, dance badly—it's a year contract, and that's that. So whatever you negotiate for, that's what you get paid. The company pays into a pension; you have the option of matching or paying in as well. Great health benefits, yeah. Awesome, awesome health benefits.

MARSHALL CRUTCHER | APRIL 2005

We have these glorious family times together that no other family might enjoy—like Mondays off. On Monday afternoon we pick James up from school, and we go to the zoo together. There's no one else around, and that's neat. Or breaks in the day. But Katita's generally working more than the average working person. That means I'm more the parent on deck, which has been a puzzle for my career, since I'm self-employed.

Katita and I have been together for twenty-one years. I met her when she was fifteen. I'm five years older; it was quite a scandal at the time. It's always been the same schedule: a forty, forty-two-week annual contract. It's very easy and comfortable during the time when they aren't in performance season. The absolute worst is tour because she's gone. That has become easier and easier as James gets older. When he was really young it was challenging for me to be working at home. That pressure on my career was tough, and I'm now coping with those issues, hoping to come out of a nosedive before Katita retires.

Katita's big fear has been stage fright. Katita doesn't like to be told what to do. I've learned that the best thing to do for her is to be extremely supportive, which is mostly just being there. So I don't talk to her before a performance, because she's in her pre-performance ritual, with her headphones. I just go, be there, sit in. Everything's taken care of, everything's calm, no crises.

Katita likes to have both emotional and physical satisfaction—she has to feel great with the partner. She really has to act the part because she's an actress as much as she's a dancer. She wants that chemistry to be working, whether the audience sees it or not. She wants to feel it and have all the technical stuff work and not be afraid.

After a performance I need to listen to what she's saying because I might have thought, "God, she nailed that! She looked so solid!" and she'll come off and say, "Eh, it was okay." However I'm feeling about the performance might be out of step. It's difficult because she wants me to be enthusiastic and positive but not wrong and insincere. So over the years, I've tended to say less and less, find out what she's really feeling after a performance. I'll ask first, "How did it go?" I won't say, "It was great." Actually, it's been better having James because he'll always come back and say, "That was beautiful, Mama; I really enjoyed it."

MARSHALL CRUTCHER | JULY 2013

In 1998 we were standing in front of Baby Gap in Laurel Village. Just standing there, for a long time. I remember thinking, "If we have another date where we go see another movie, I'm going to barf." We had been doing that for a long time. We'd kind of worn it out. We'd done the Monday Night Football with friends. We'd done the travel with the company. We'd done all of our "couple life" together. It just felt…hollow.

There's a very narrow window in the San Francisco Ballet schedule, so we thought, "Wow, how do we engineer this?" Because Katita was almost thirty; she knew that if she were away for a long period of time, she'd fall off the dance card. If Katita could get pregnant in November or December, then when the summer break happened, she could have a child during the layoff and then maybe take a little bit of time off and come back for *Nutcracker*. Then back in full swing because she was sometimes dancing eighteen roles a year.

James was born August 16, 1999. Katita started breast-feeding and getting ready to go back to work, and she lost absolutely all of her weight. By the time it was October—two months later—we were over at the park, and everyone thought we'd adopted because she was rail thin again. She was trying to breast-feed and dance at the same time. She should have been eating more. Well, I tried.

We were really afraid that having a child would hurt Katita's career, and it did the opposite. It gave her a little bit of a parent's perspective about taking a step back from the rat race of trying to be Helgi's favorite for this role or that role. That didn't matter as much anymore. She was able to relax a little bit, to work hard for herself instead of someone else, to improve her teaching, to teach herself. Three or four years after she had James, people were saying to her, "My God, where did you come from? You're better than before!" That's a rare story.

Some of that was her own physiology. But it was also that she had taken this break, this time to heal, and had seen how she could come back to work in a way that was smart. That was a big boon.

James was at the ballet quite a bit because we try to connect as much as possible when Katita is busy. The ballet becomes a node for us getting together. Maybe if Katita can't come home, I can go there with him. Or we'll share a car ride down. I'll do something with James, and then I'll come back and pick her up when her rehearsal's done. We'll have dinner together, then she'll go back down and finish the day. If it's *Nutcracker*, maybe we can go a couple times a week—we can check out the set, and we'll hang out backstage. Maybe we'll see the first act. Dress rehearsals are brilliant for little kids because everybody's talking a little bit in the audience anyway, and as long as we don't distract the choreographers and the production people, heck, we can even sit in the front row because it's kind of loud by the orchestra, and he gets to see all of the instruments. A lot of repertory is short, which is great for little kids. *Carnival of the Animals*, *Rodeo*, *Don Quixote*. At least once a season there were one or two ballets where I thought, "He'd like the first act," or, "There are lots of great costumes, so we can circle around backstage and see how they are made and go downstairs and see all the fuss and muss of the wigs." He grew up down there; all the people know him. The makeup people, the wig people, the costume people. He grew up trying on hats.

Katita rehearsed roles with him. She would dance with him and talk about the roles, talk about make-believe and presenting yourself onstage. He started dancing in the *Nutcracker*. He was the littlest boy in the party scene. It was Katita's last *Nutcracker* and his first ballet ever, and they overlapped and got to dance on the same stage together. That was fantastic.

KATITA WALDO | JULY 2013

I retired three years ago, and then came out of retirement briefly in May. Now I'm back in retirement, as far as I know. I still perform, even though I'm retired; I will occasionally do character parts. This year I must have made close to $7,000 or $8,000 in addition to my salary. At my height—the last two, three years that I was dancing—I was also doing ballet mastering. Just as a dancer, I was making over $100,000 a year. When I was doing double-duty, I think, in my final years, I made $120,000, something like that. And I now make $73,000 to $75,000 a year, then extra for performances and for teaching. For about twenty to thirty classes a year, I get between $70 and $150 per class (not just here, but at other companies). I have nothing but gratitude for everyone. Throughout my career there have been highs and lows here and there, and the company's always tried their best to help me in any way they can. I've gotten loans, cash advances, just everything and anything that would help.

I am a ballet master, which is kind of like being a coach or director in a stage play—not like the director of a company. You learn the ballets that choreographers come in and set. You're in charge of making sure that the ballets are put together. You make sure new dancers know their parts. If it's been a long time, you might be the one who re-teaches the ballet to the company. We have the same schedule, essentially, as the dancers. But we don't get the breaks that the dancers get, because the ballet masters aren't union. I'm now on the managerial side, so I always joke, "Now I get to tell *them* what to do." But the truth is, yeah, now I *have* to tell them what to do. Before, they were my friends. We could bitch together, complain about this and that. We were all looking at things from the same perspective. Now that I'm on the other side, there are some elements that were what I thought they were: that the director just likes this person more than this other person. But strangely, there's a lot less of that than I thought there was. There are *all* sorts of reasons that have to do with logistics and practicality and availability for who gets to do what and why they get to do it. A lot of it just has to do with (from Helgi's perspective): "I have seventy-something dancers, and I want them all to dance." Of course, all of us have favorites. If I were director, I would pick the ones that I liked. And that's hard to accept—when you feel that you're not to somebody's taste. But that's kind of how it goes. I think that that's the hardest thing for dancers to accept.

It hurts. You'll look at a dancer—I know this, having been a dancer myself—and you'll see that you can technically do the part more efficiently or better or with more strength. And you don't understand why this person is getting the part when they fall out of their pirouettes or they can't do thirty-two fouettés. When I was a dancer I don't think that I was as open as I am now to seeing what a person has onstage. Now I think, "Well, my God! OK, the legs don't go up, but, Jesus! She comes onstage and she's stunning! She's beautiful! She has this quality." And I didn't appreciate that before, because I was being competitive. You look at yourself in the mirror 24-7, and the whole point is to get the parts you want. So that's all you're thinking about: I want to get the part. Why can't I get the part?

The hardest issues to deal with in this art form are weight and age. It's really hard because, as an artist, you're reaching your peak when your body is starting to slow down. Sometimes it's got nothing to do with your technical ability; you are dancing better than you ever have. But your body has changed its shape. It's not even that you're fat at all. It's that you've just suddenly changed. With women, you lose your waist a bit. I never had one to begin with, but then it just goes! And you get a little wider, and the thing that made you youthful, it's just not there. The argument is, "Well, why is that a bad thing?" Well, it isn't a bad thing. But whether you like it or not, you don't want to see Juliet played by a forty-year-old. I know that a beautiful, magnificent, incredible actress can do it. I know that Margot Fonteyn at sixty was mesmerizing. But how many Margot Fonteyns are there out there, really?

As far as I'm concerned, coming back from having a baby is the same as coming back from having an injury. It feels so cruel because you have to prove yourself all over again. I came back from being pregnant, and I felt as though

Helgi hated me—he'd forgotten about me. I made myself suffer more than I needed to because I looked at it as punishment for having had a baby. But it's not personal. Does it happen that sometimes the boss decides he likes the person who did your part better? Yeah. Does it suck if it happens to you? Yes. But is it wrong? No, it isn't.

It was Marshall who did everything, pretty much, with James. Had James gone into ballet, I might have been more of the activity parent. But he went into baseball, and I don't like baseball, and Marshall adores baseball. So they go off and do baseball. And I like a lot of alone time. At times I wish that I could be more like Marshall: more present with James, more in the moment, more aware of everything that he's doing. But the truth is that I'm just not that kind of person. I am private, and I'm quiet; I'm like a cat.

But I think that I have something very special with my son that I'm very proud of, and it makes me very happy. He has my sense of humor. I love seeing who he's becoming. There's very little that he could ever say to me that would offend me. I am thrilled that he feels comfortable sharing with me things that I know his peers would rather die than share with their parents. I was like that with my parents, and it means so much to me that they're the people I can go to. I can always trust them, and I think James feels the same. I love that. I love that he still hugs me and he still kisses me.

MARSHALL CRUTCHER | MAY 2014

We bought our house in 1999 for $350,000. We sold our house in 2012. Our story arc as artists in San Francisco was that once the tech bubble initially popped after 9/11, and then we hit the recession of 2008, and Katita retired in 2010 and her salary was diminished, that was one bridge too far. When we had James, it was an up time in the economy, and I was working for Disney doing games and for other corporate clients. The first two years of James's life turned out to be the busiest years of my life, professionally—on top of Katita being away, traveling with the company. Once you're holding a baby and trying to get

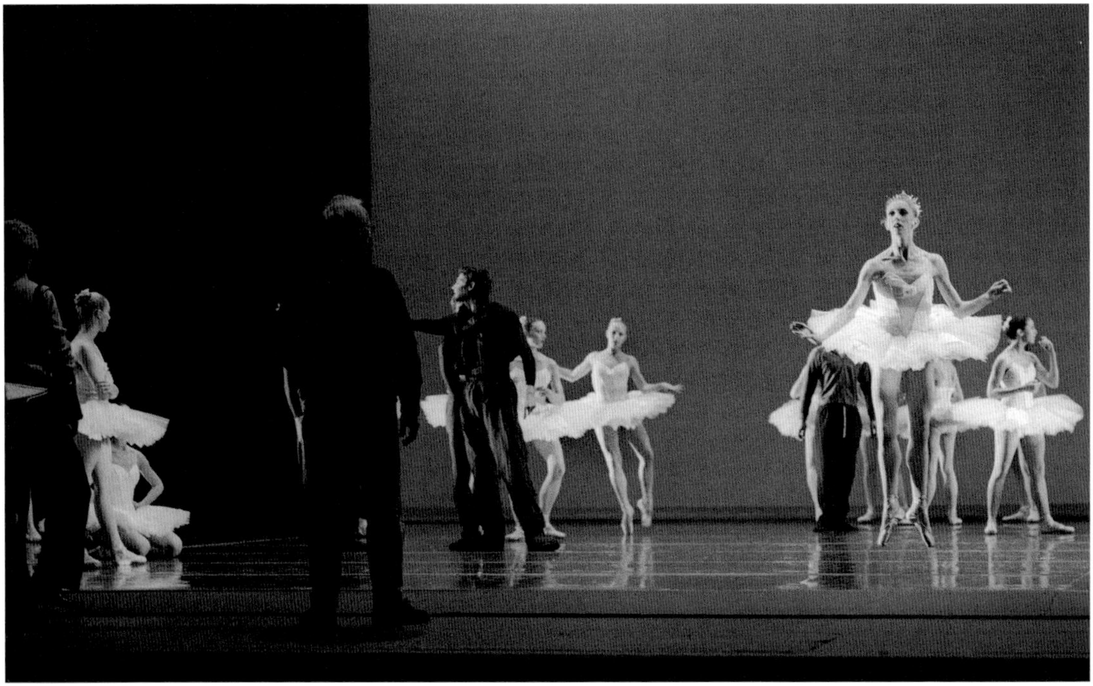

The company rests during a dress rehearsal—all but Katita, who wants Helgi's attention. She keeps dancing. He notices. Then he turns away, and she is devastated. (2001)

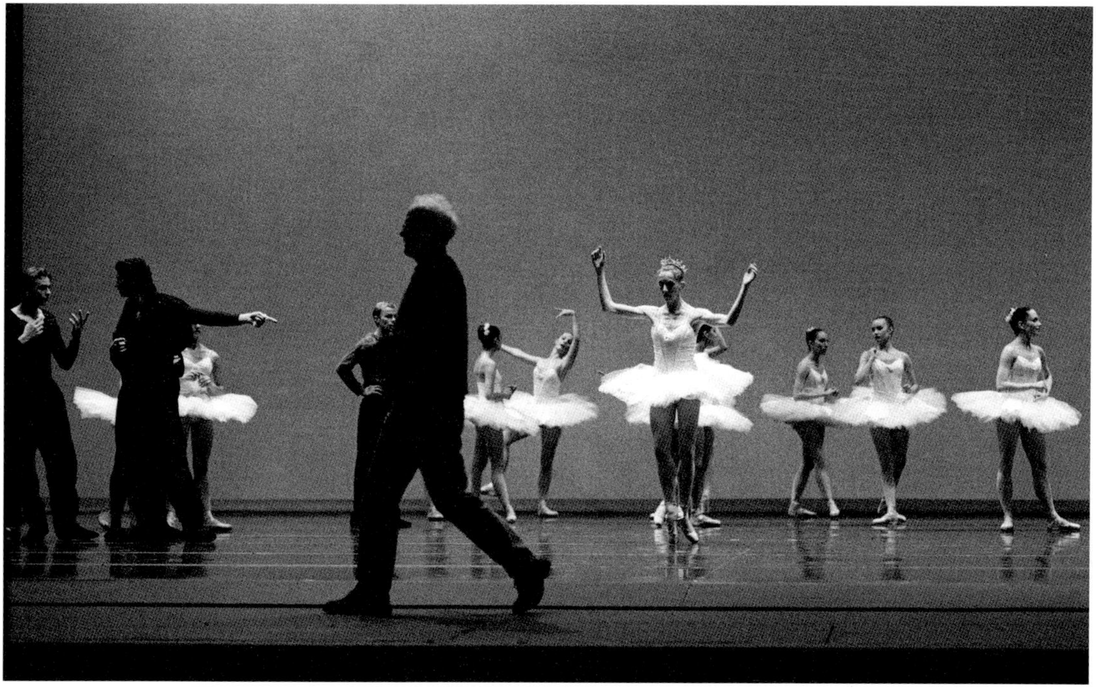

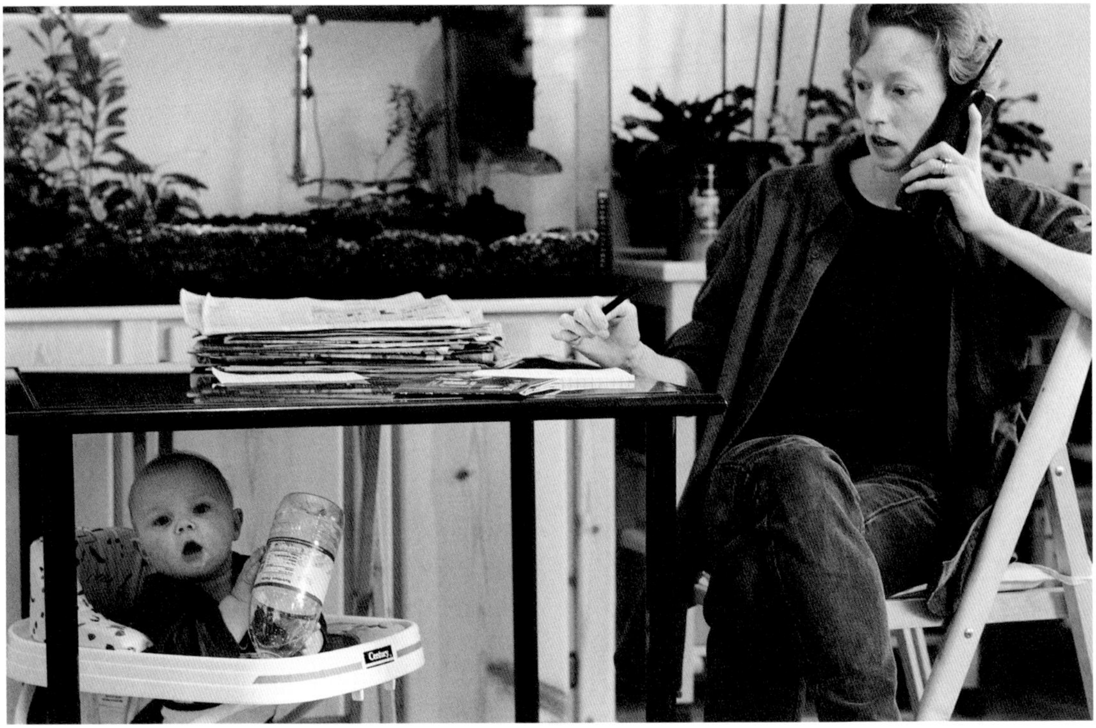

above
Katita at home making cold calls for Marshall's business while James plays. (2001)

top right
Katita and James at Safeway market on Twenty-Fourth Street in San Francisco. (2001)

bottom right
Katita puts James in his car seat. (2001)

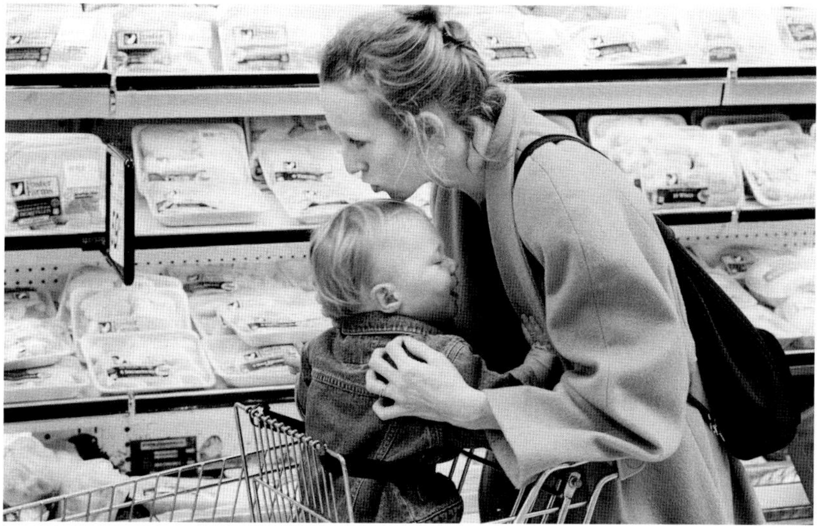

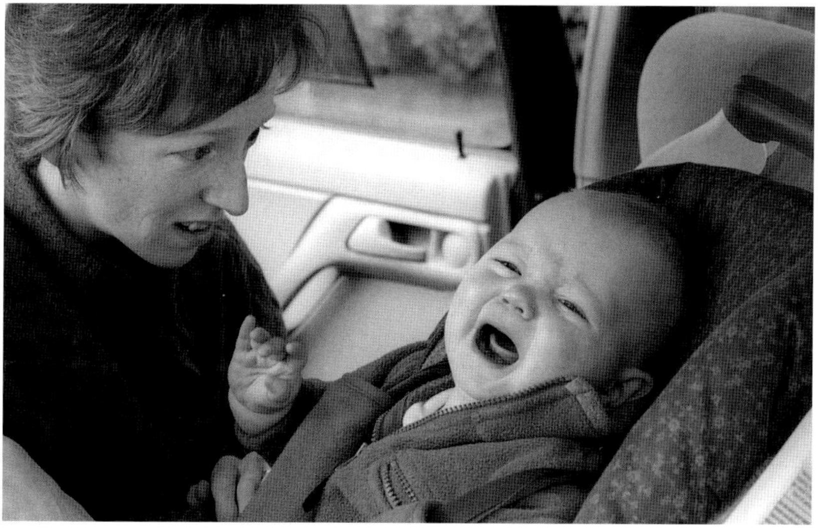

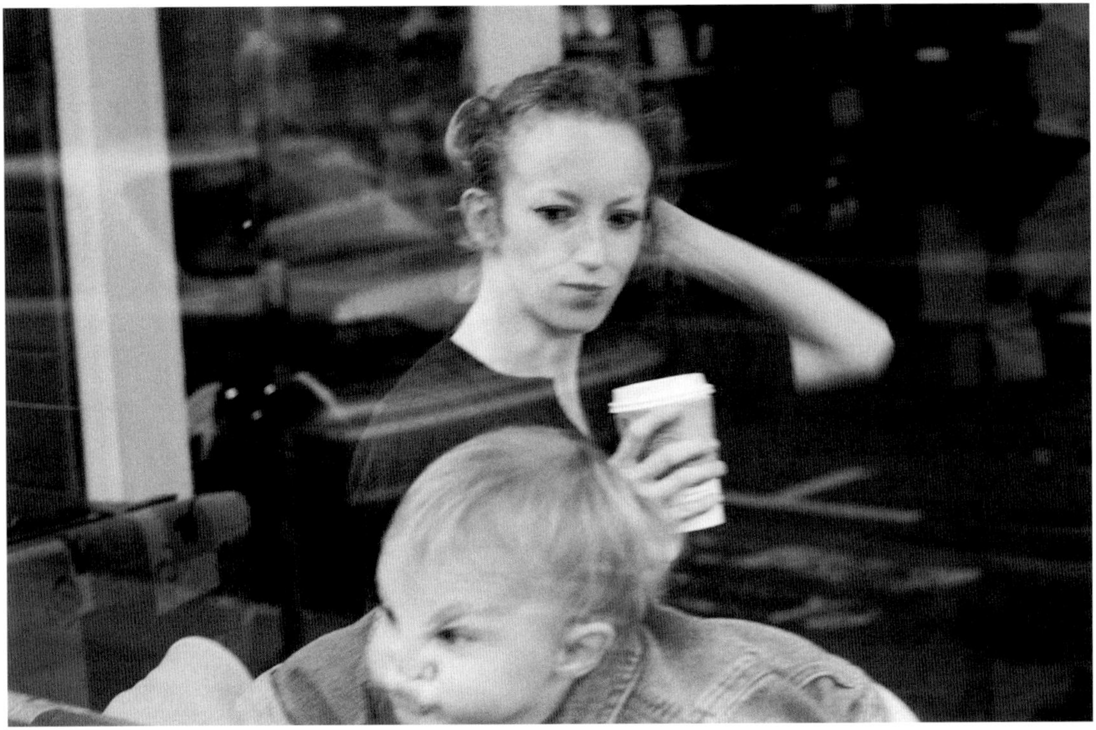

Katita and James at Starbucks for lunch. At day care he has cried until he turned blue and passed out on three occasions. His caregivers have needed to call an ambulance each time, and Katita has just been told that he cannot return. After his parents find another day care, he never cries quite like that again. (2002)

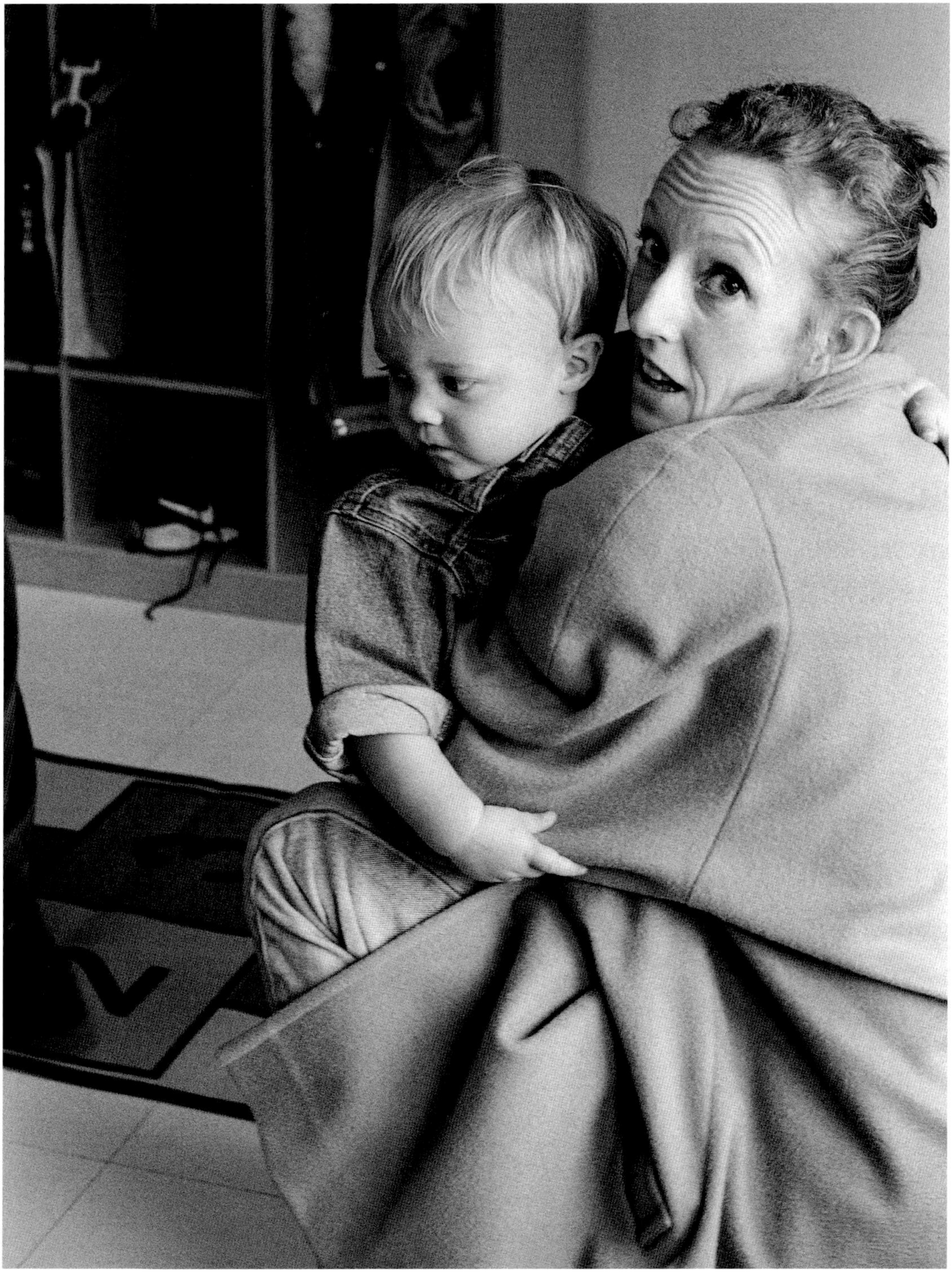

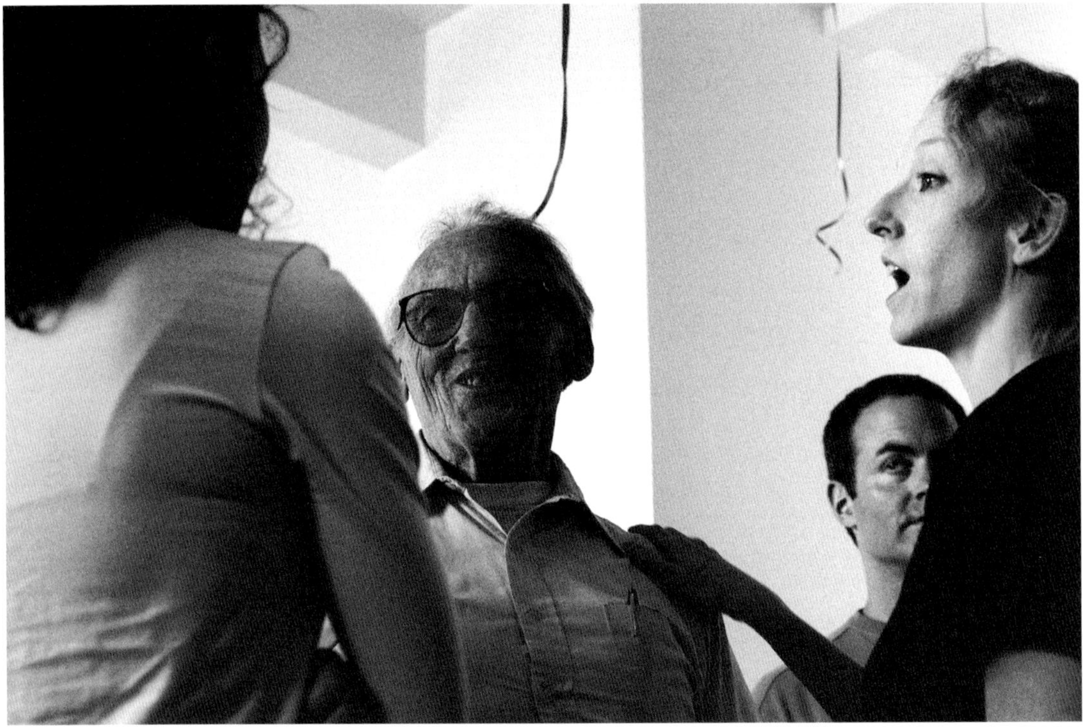

Kristin, Graham Waldo (Katita's father), Marshall Crutcher (Katita's husband), and Katita at a joint birthday party for Kai and James, at Michael and Kristin's apartment in San Francisco. (2000)

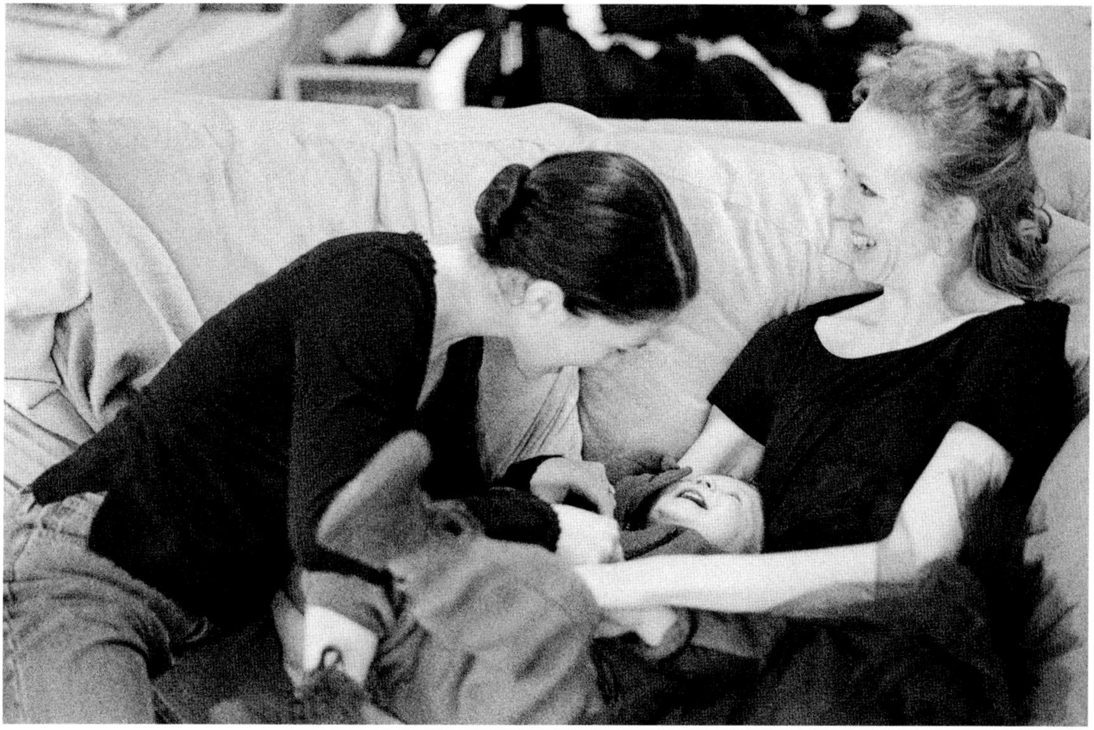

Kristin and Katita tickle James in the company lounge. (2002)

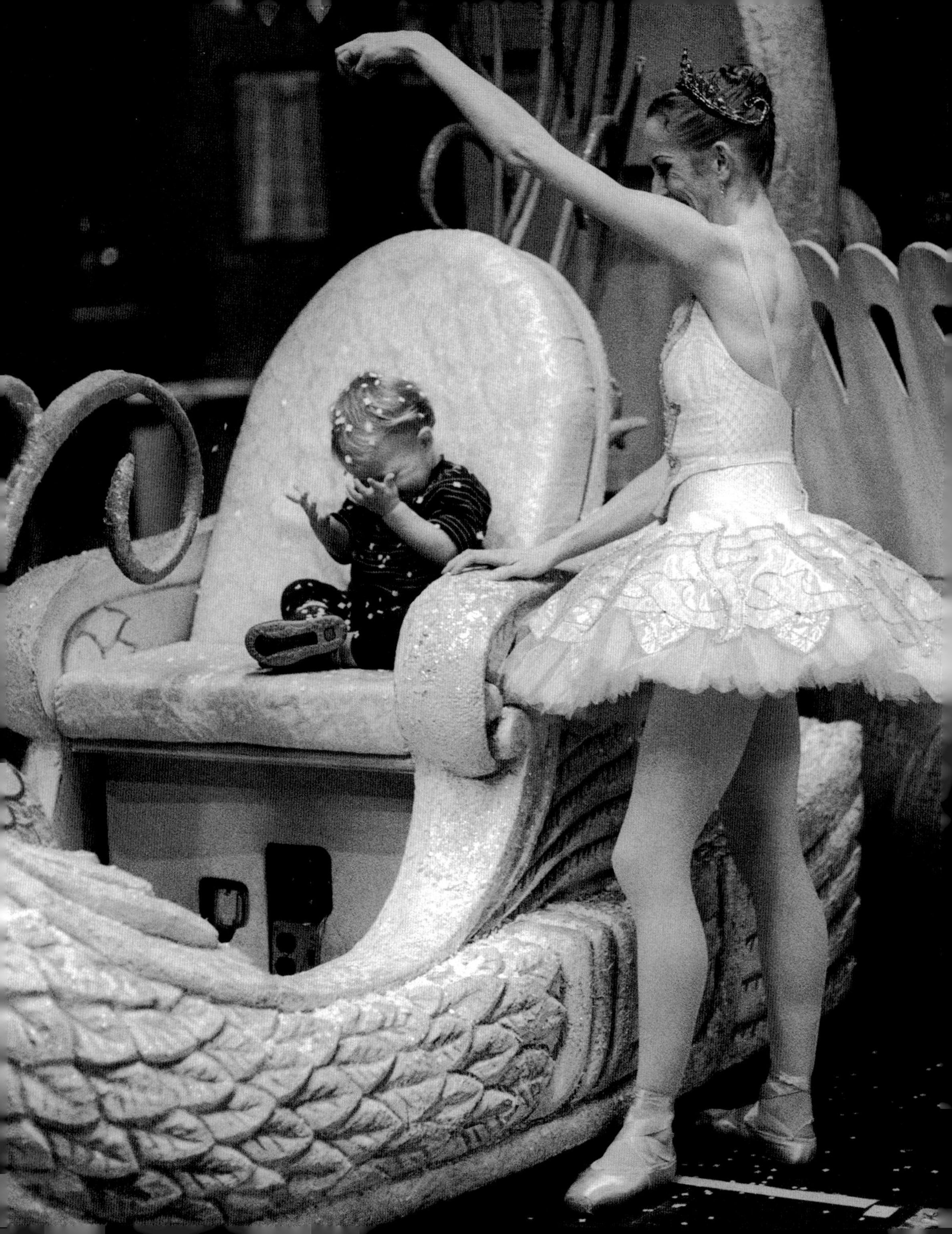

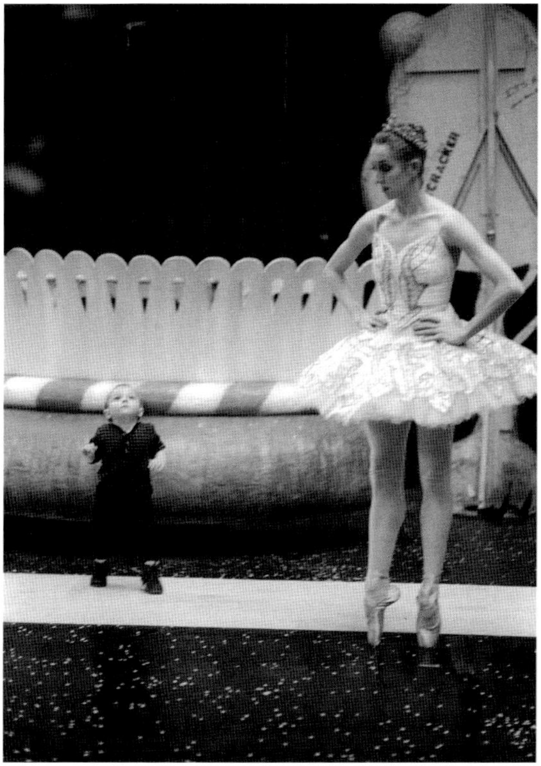

James and Katita backstage after a performance of *Nutcracker Ballet* (Marius Petipa). (2001)

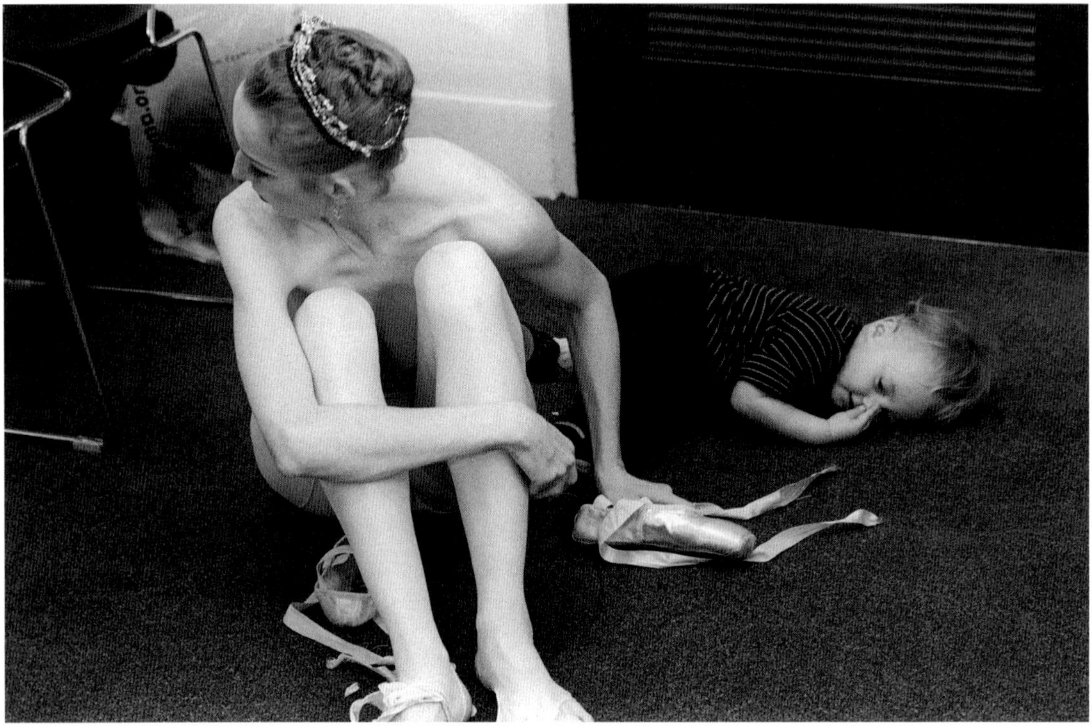

In her dressing room after a performance of *Nutcracker Ballet*, Katita clowns with James. She is so thin at this point that she hears Helgi is worried about her. (2001)

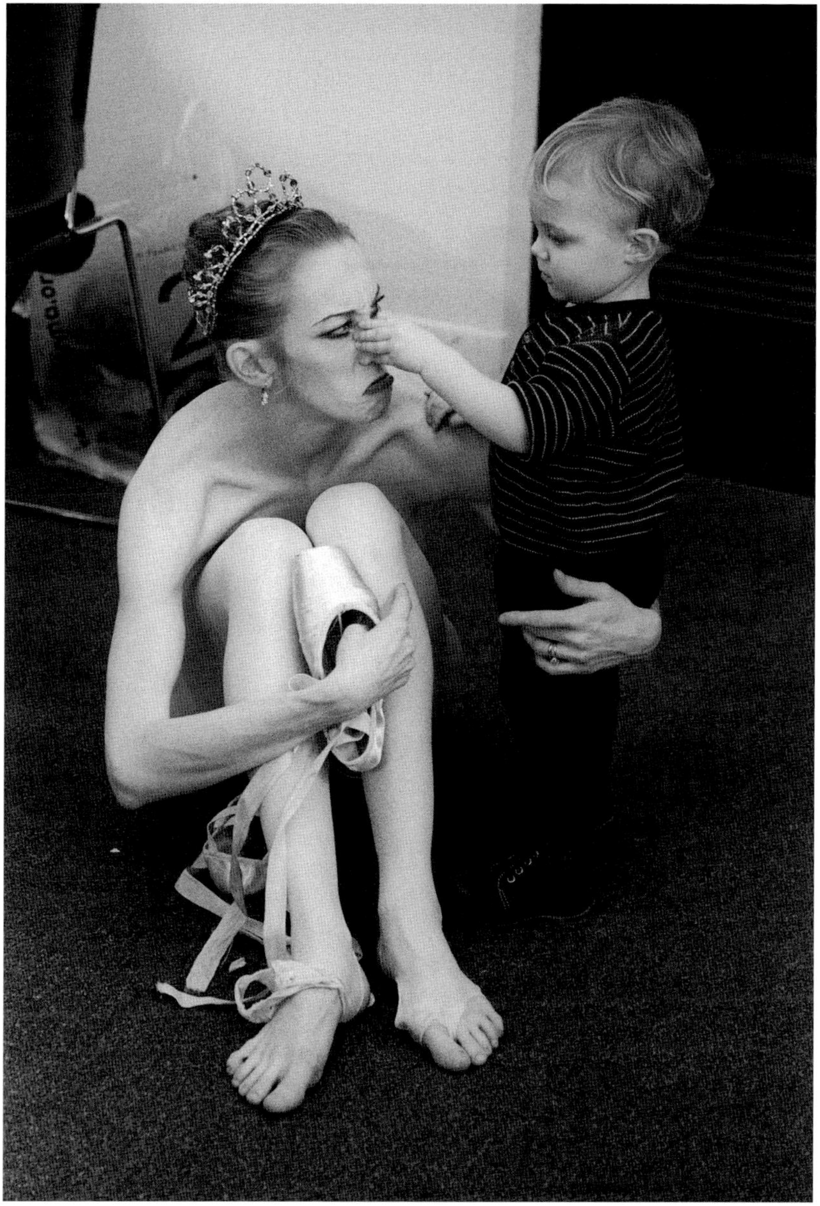

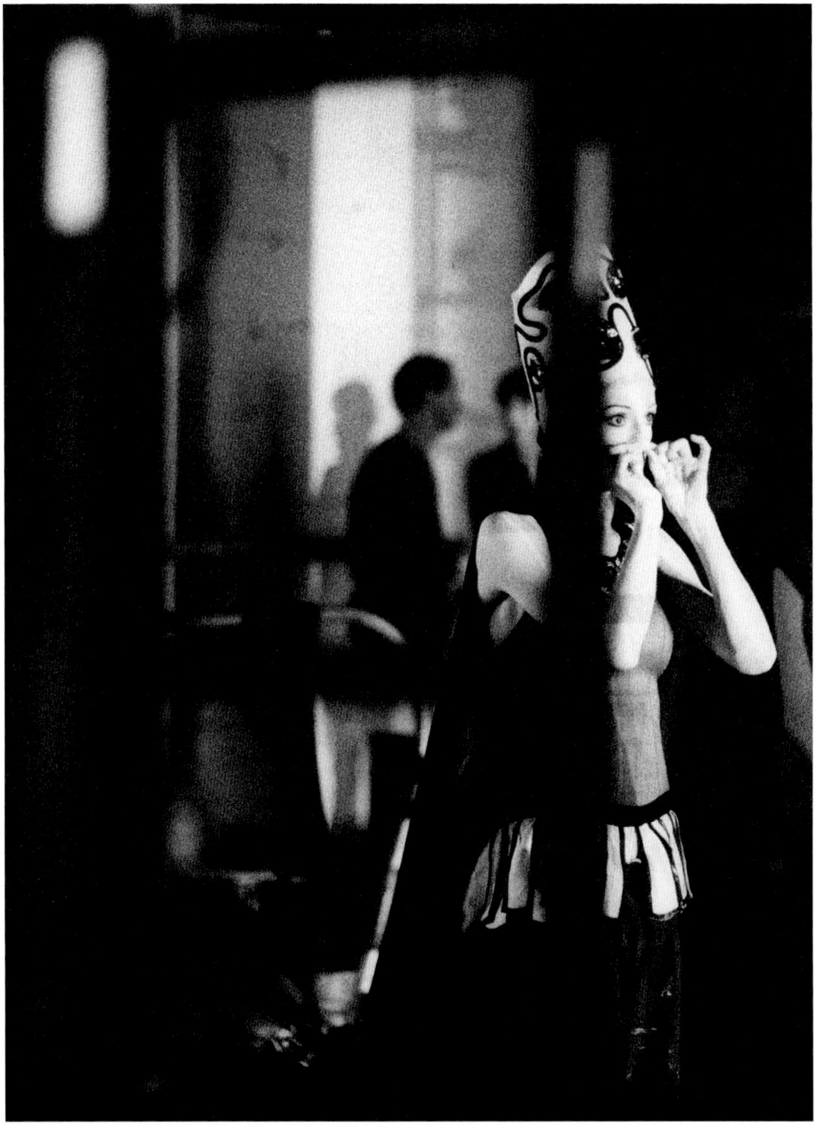

Katita about to perform *Prodigal Son* (George Balanchine). She has stage fright; Helgi is in the house, and this performance will affect her casting for the rest of the season. (2002)

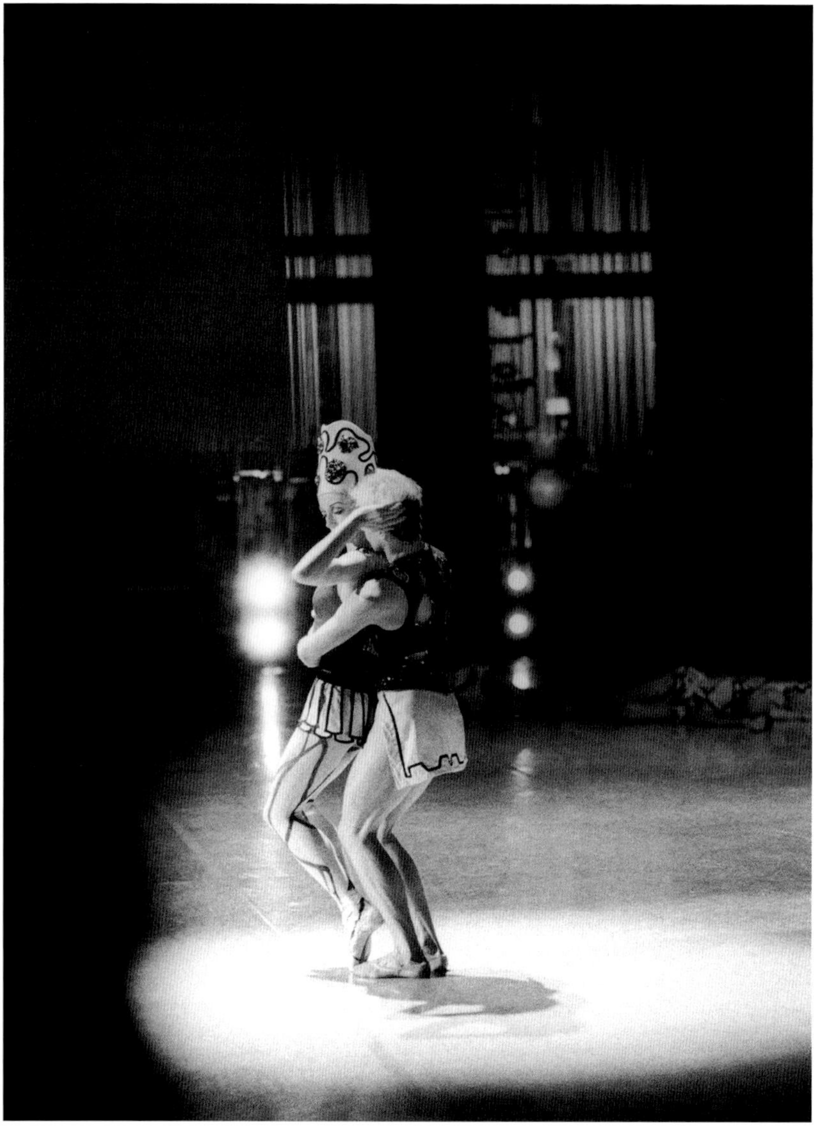

Katita and Gennadi Nedvigin dance the principal roles in *Prodigal Son*. (2002)

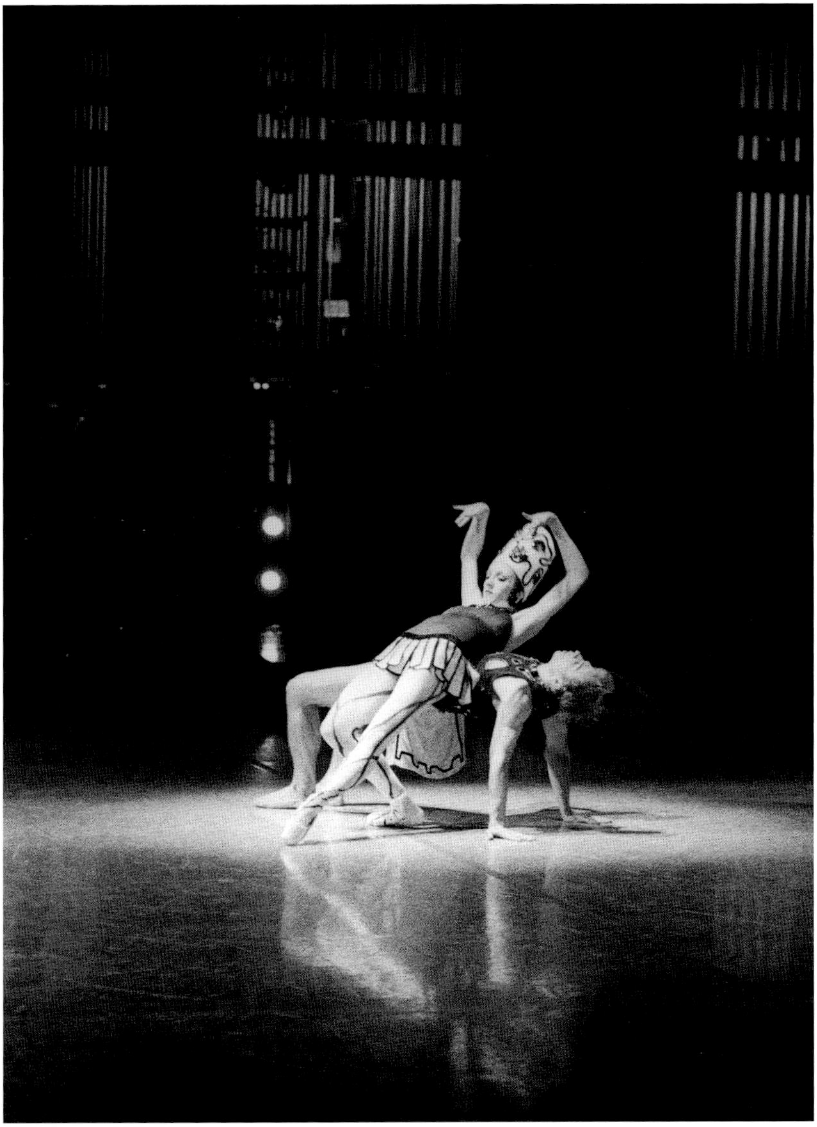

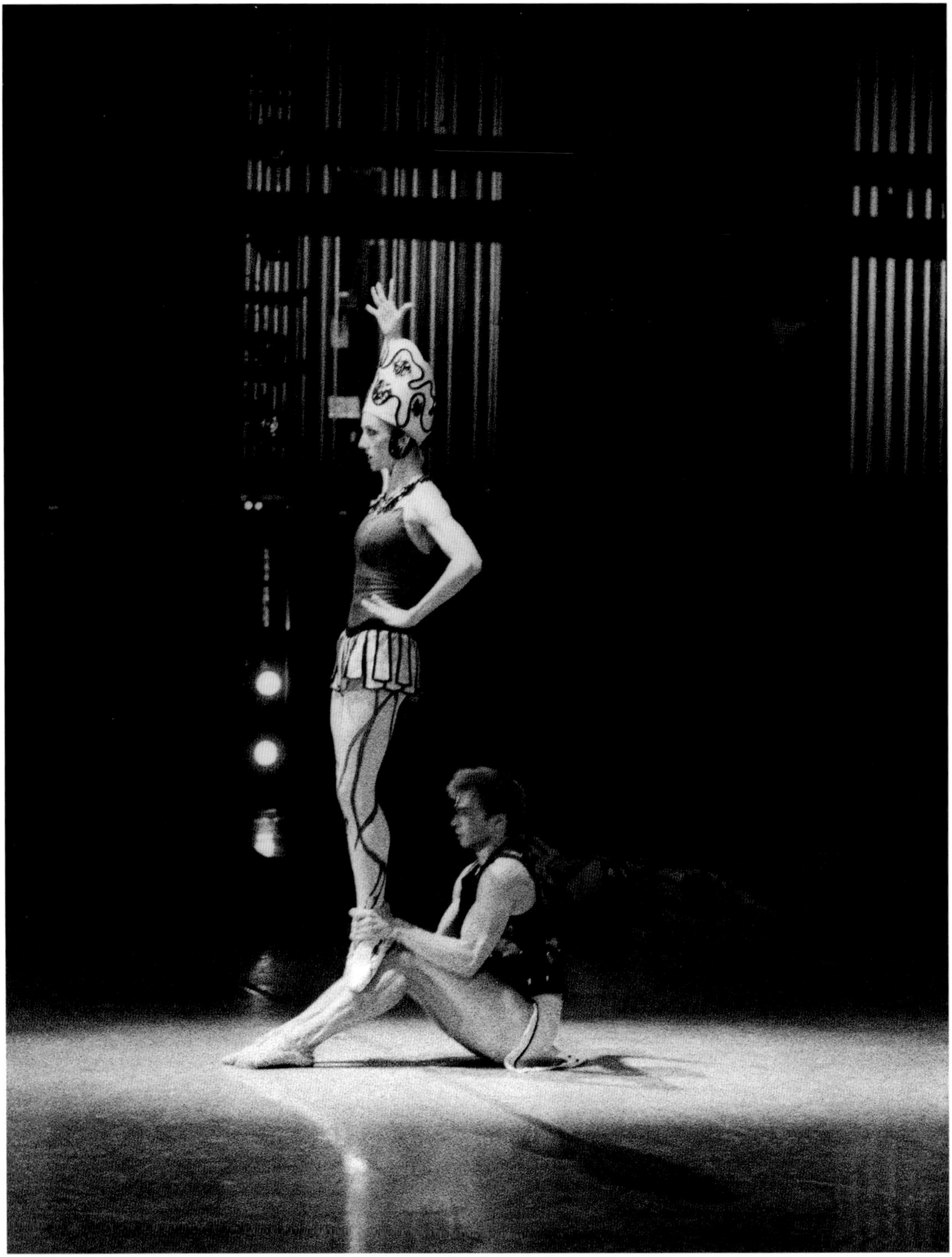

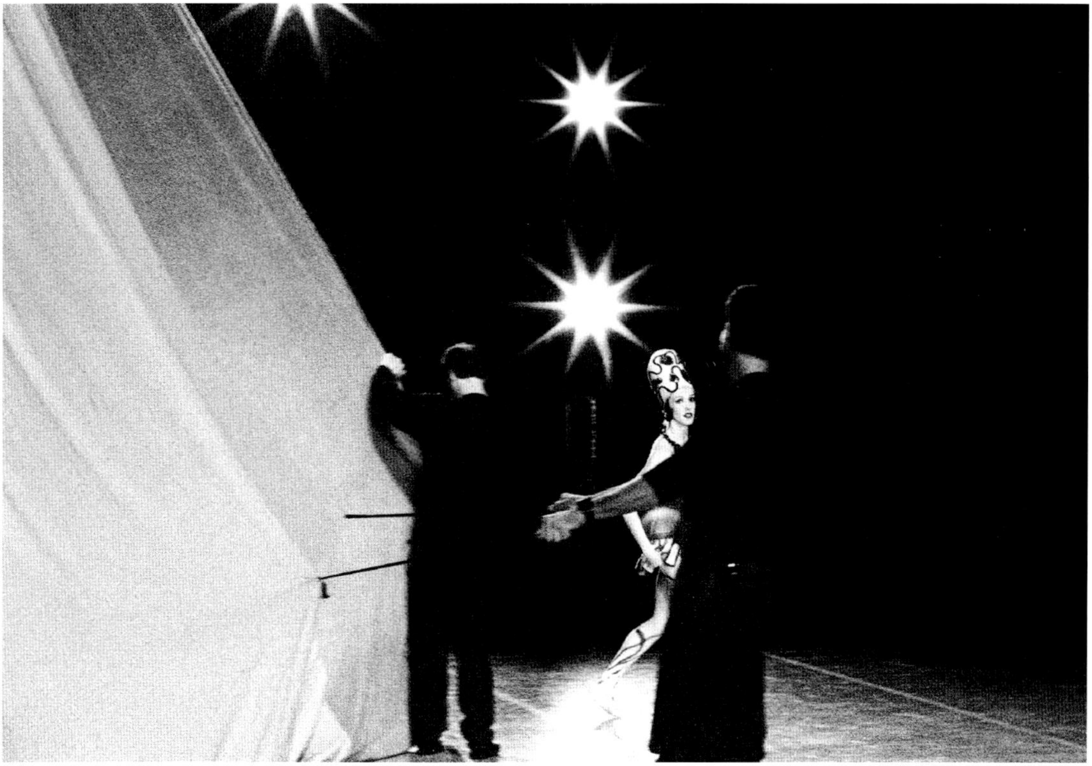

Katita backstage between three curtain calls after her performance of *Prodigal Son*. (2002)

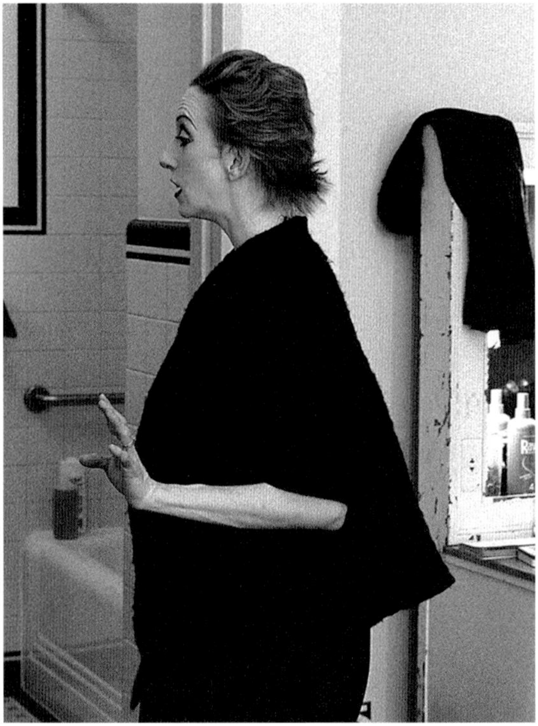

Katita in her dressing room after performing *Prodigal Son*; she has heard that Helgi thinks her performance was weak. She is terrified that she may lose the job she needs in order to support her family. (2002)

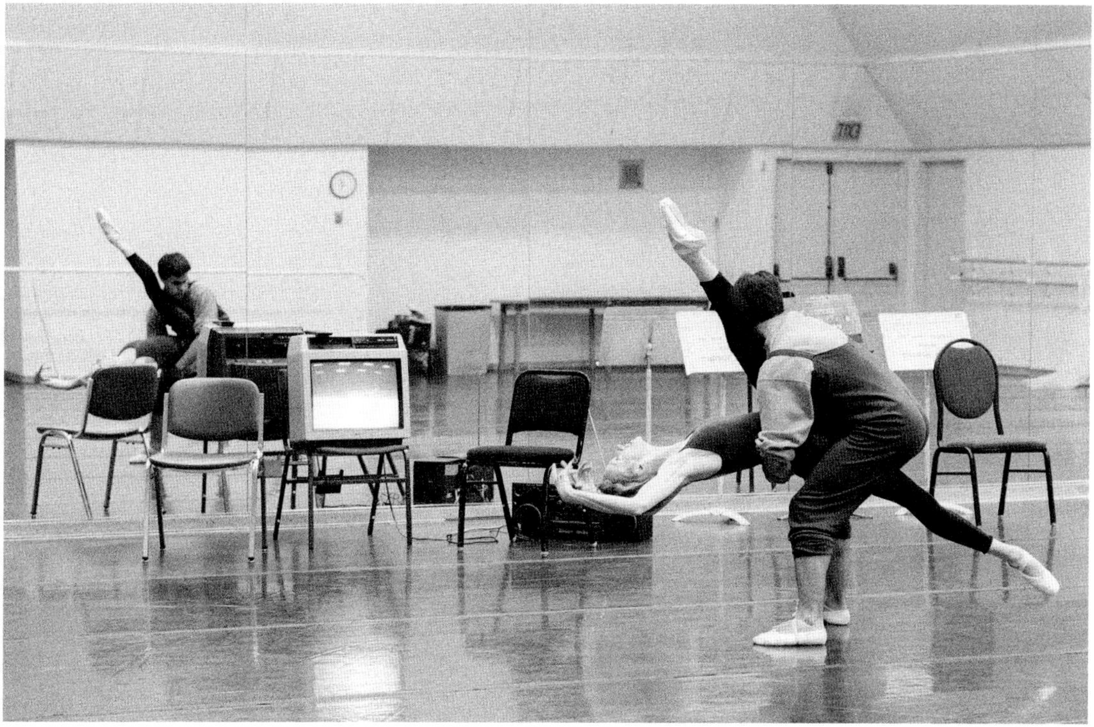

Katita and Joan Boada rehearse for *Bugaku* (George Balanchine). (2000)

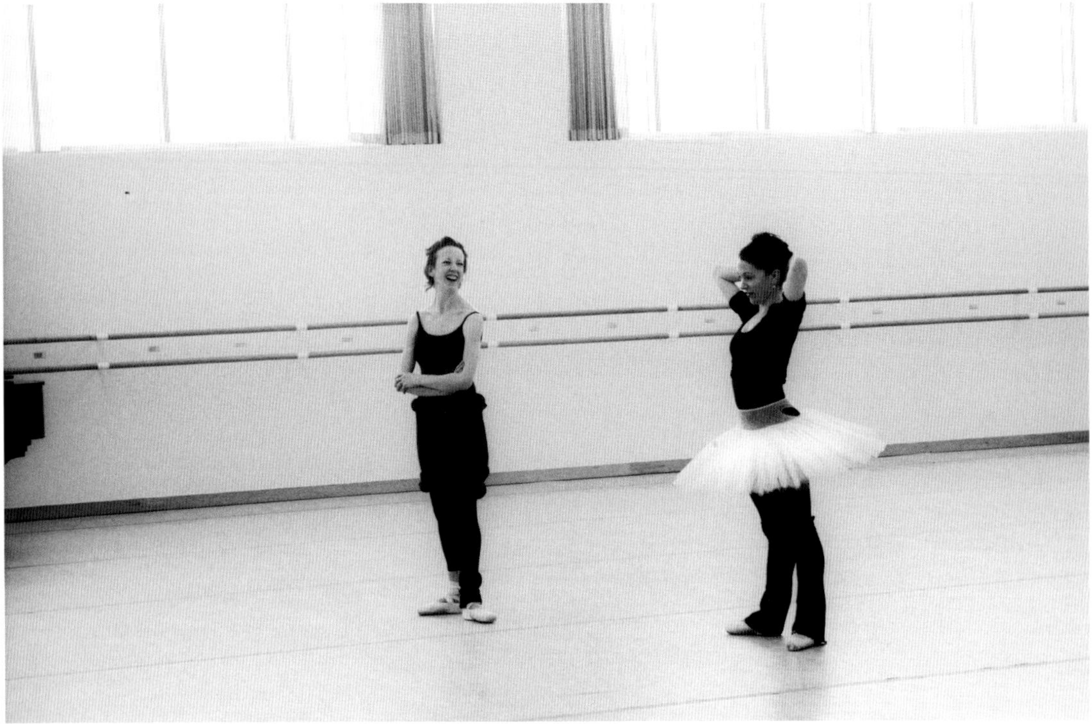

above

Katita is a jokester, while Kristin tends to be in her own world. (2000)

right

James and Katita in the hall outside James's dressing room before they perform in *Nutcracker Ballet* (Helgi Tomasson). She advises him how to handle himself onstage. (2007)

overleaf

James, now in street clothes, has come to Katita's dressing room after their performance in *Nutcracker Ballet*. He is listed as a dancer in the program! (2007)

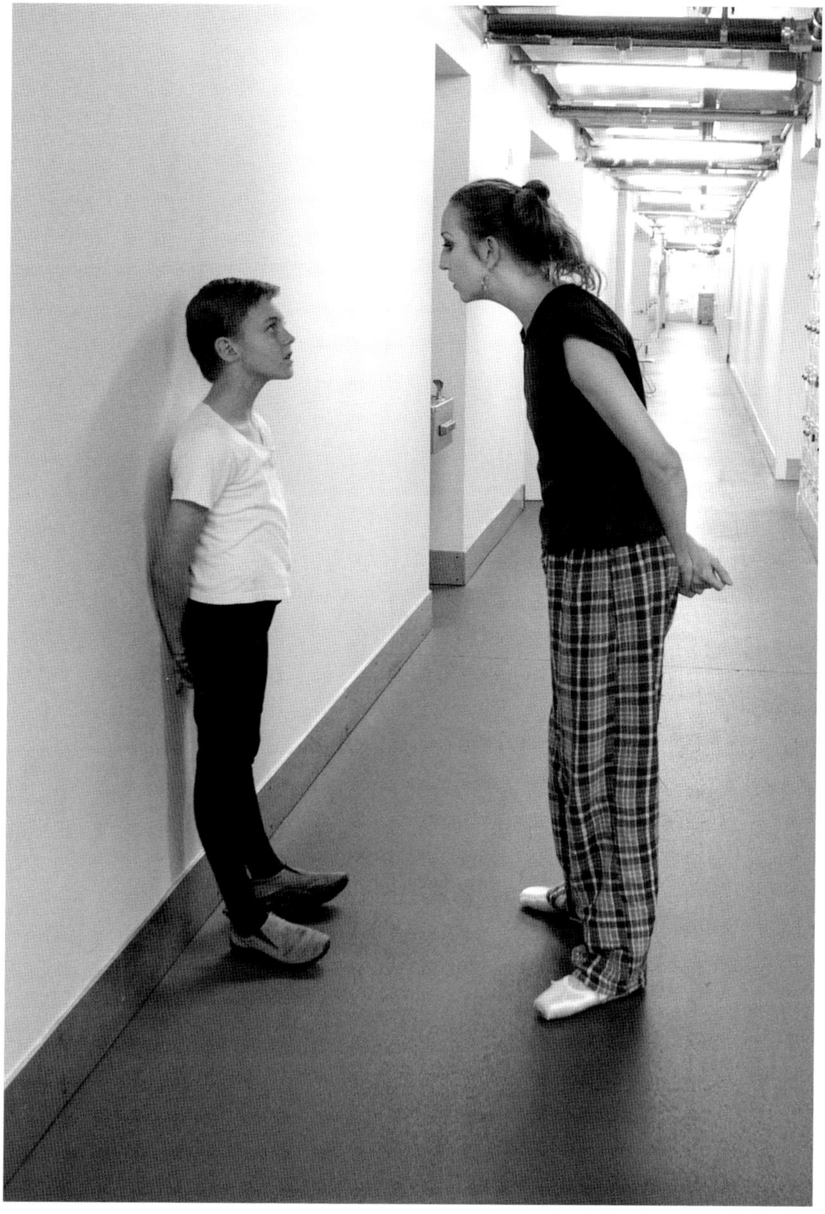

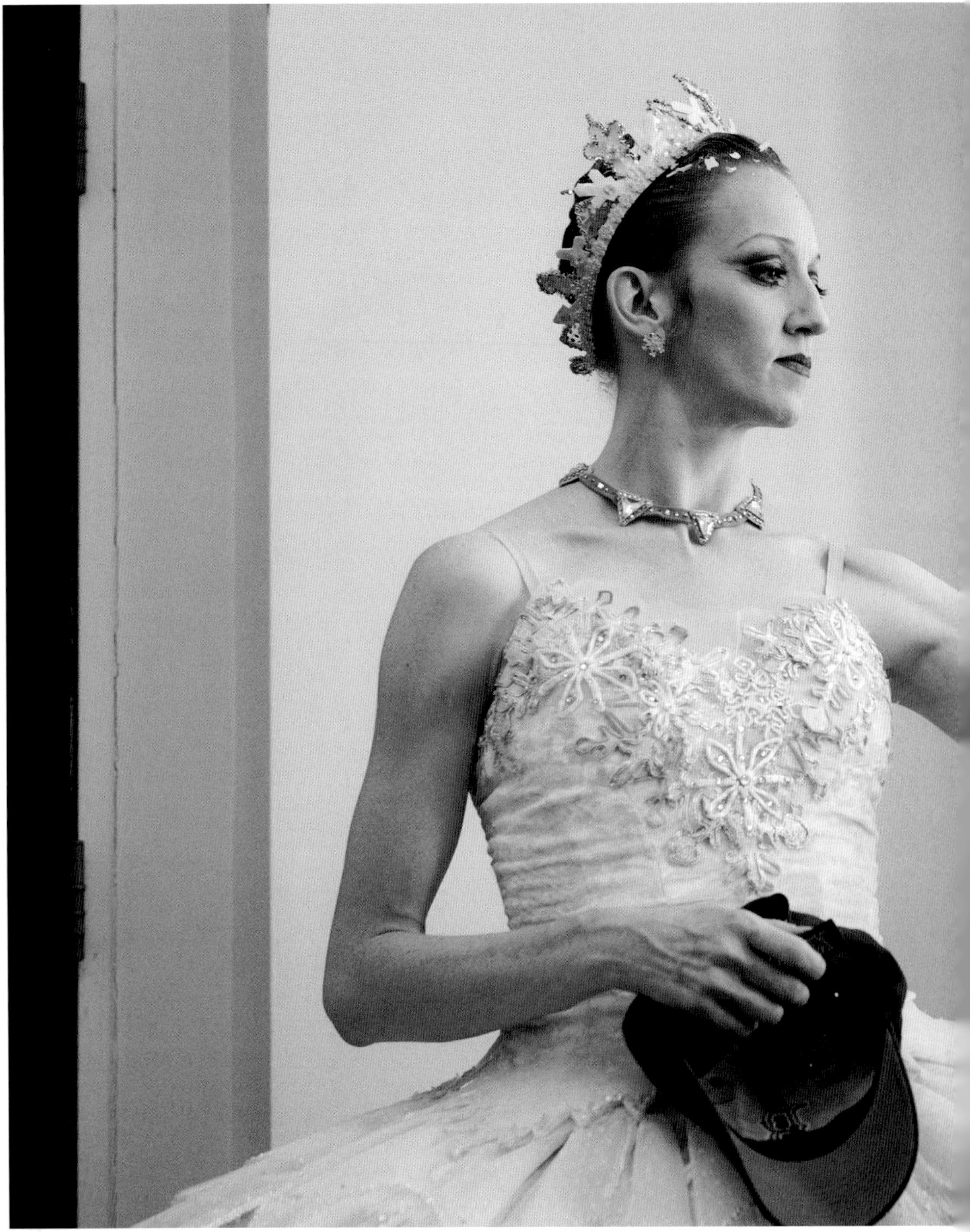

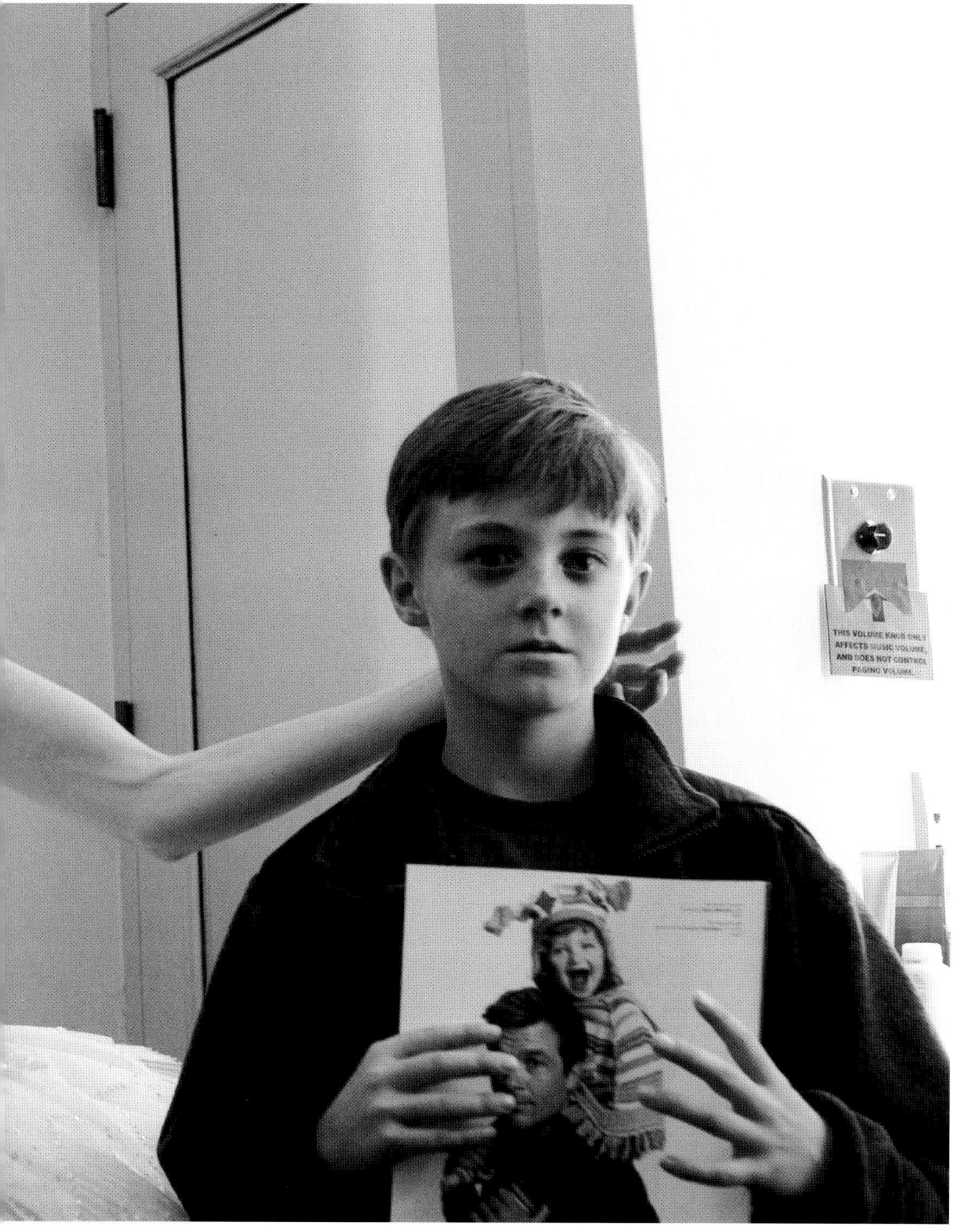
THIS VOLUME KNOB ONLY
AFFECTS MUSIC VOLUME,
AND DOES NOT CONTROL
PAGING VOLUME.

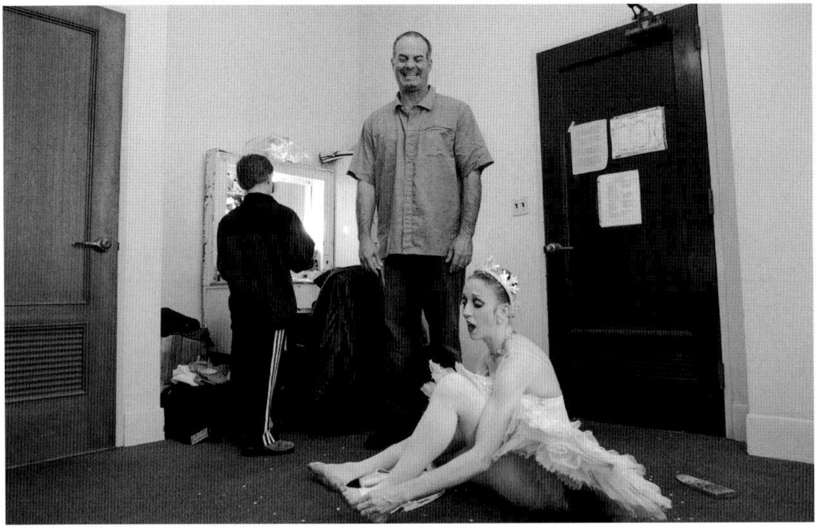

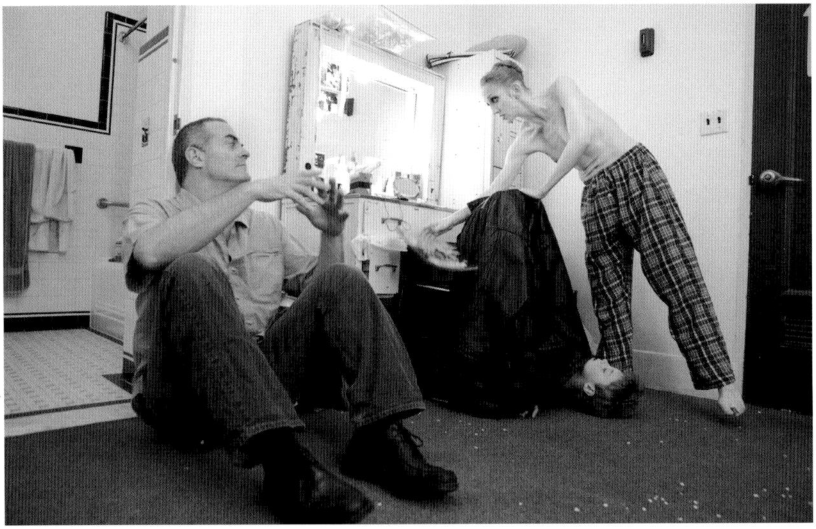

James wants to play ping-pong in the basement of the ballet while Katita is dressing. Marshall says no, and there has been a fight with tears. The white specks on the ground are fake snowflakes from the performance, carried in on Katita's tutu. (2007)

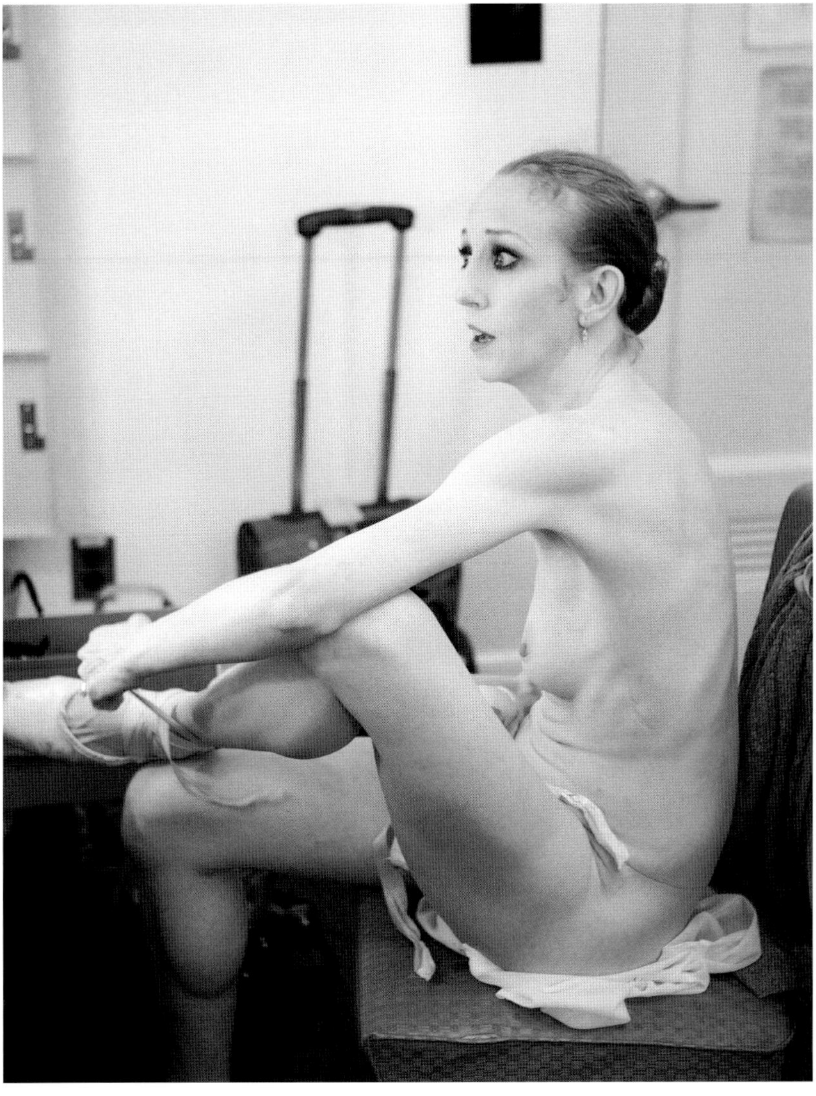

In her dressing room, Katita takes off her ballet slipper after her final performance. (2010)

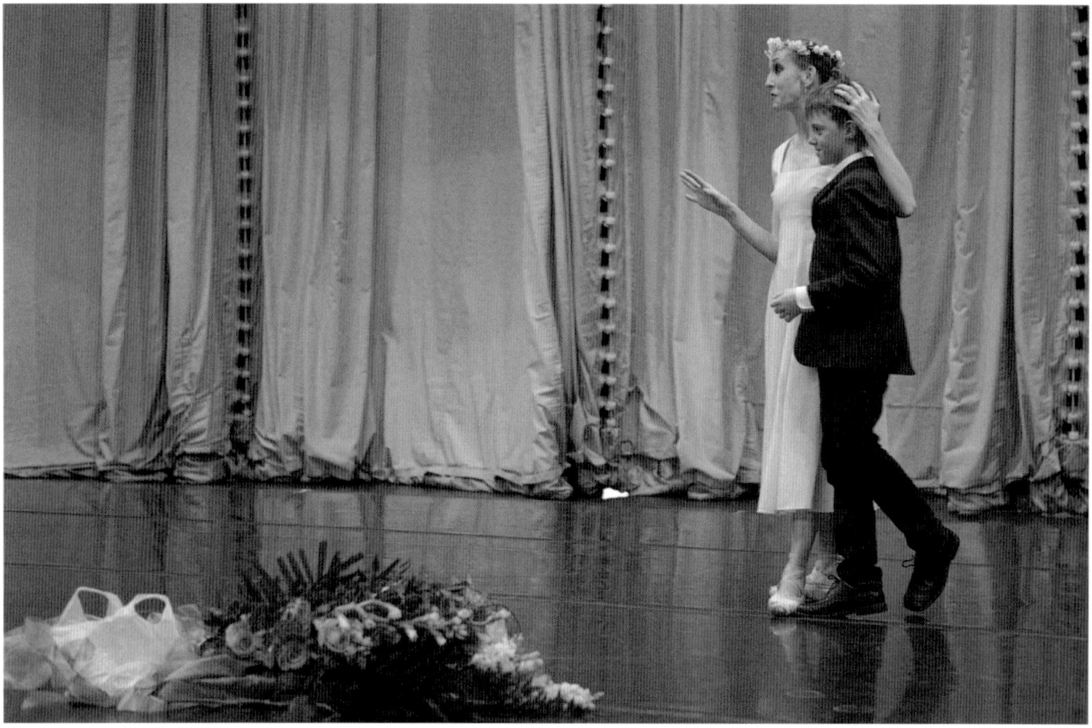

Katita and James after the curtain has come down on the night she is retiring as a dancer at the San Francisco Ballet. The flowers in the foreground were thrown onstage from the audience when she took her final bow. (2010)

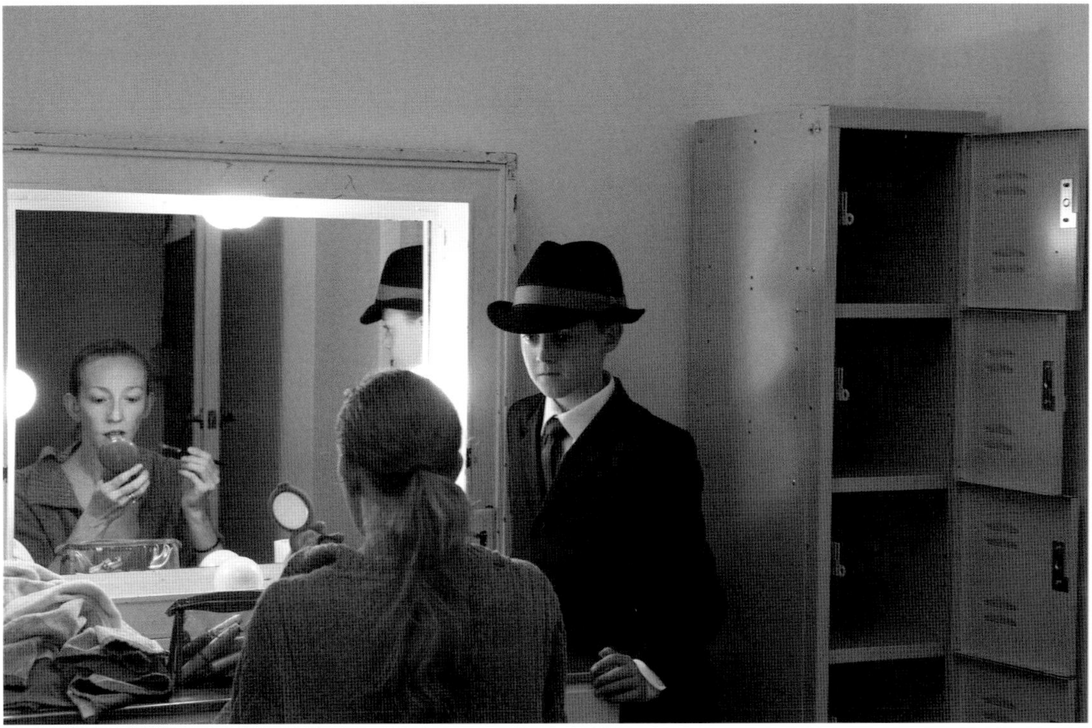

James watches Katita get ready for her retirement dinner at the nearby Hayes Street Grill. Her dressing room is now empty of her belongings, which Marshall is taking to their car. (2010)

right
The lobby of the War Memorial Opera House during dress rehearsal; Katita tells James a funny story. (2014)

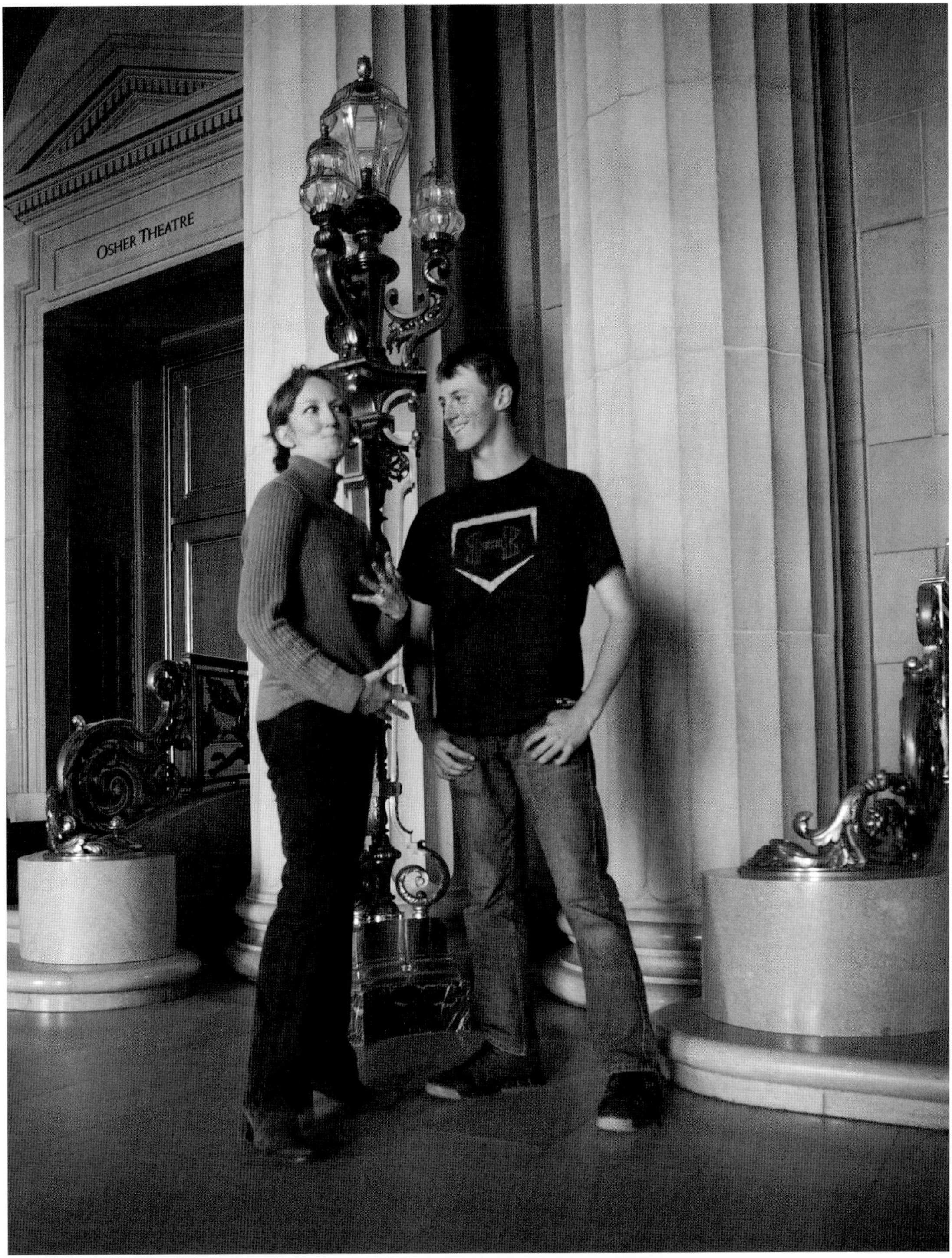
OSHER THEATRE

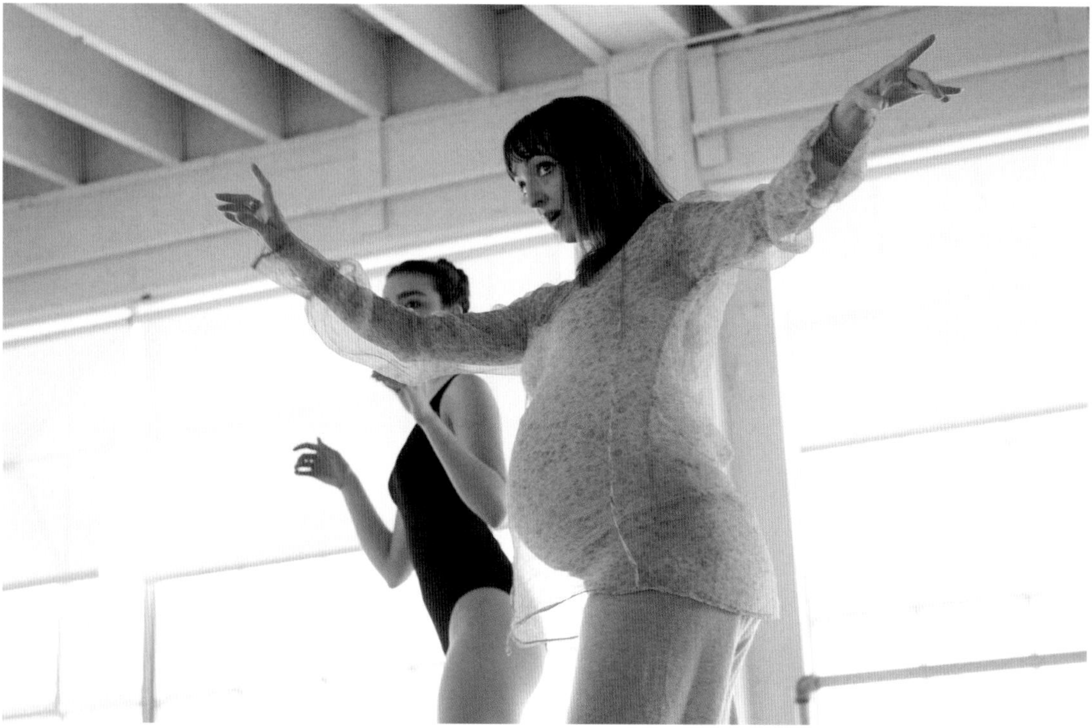

above
Lorena Feijoo had long dreamed of having a child. Less than a week before she has her baby, she gives a private lesson. (2012)

overleaf
One week before the birth of her baby girl, Luciana, Lorena dances with her partner, Vitor Luiz, in Muir Woods, California. (2012)

EPILOGUE

LORENA FEIJOO

Lorena Feijoo was trained at the National Ballet School of Cuba in her hometown of Havana. She joined San Francisco Ballet in 1999 as a principal dancer, the same year this project began. She said from the start that she wanted to be in the book—she wanted to be a mom. Meanwhile, Feijoo won an Isadora Duncan Dance Award in 2003, and she has danced as a guest at the Bolshoi Ballet in Moscow; American Ballet Theater in New York; and on television in *Great Performances: Dance in Americas* (2003), *Sesame Street* (2008), and *Dancing with the Stars* (2011). She also appeared in Andy Garcia's feature film *The Lost City* (2005). At last, in 2012, when she was forty, her dream came true and she had a baby girl, Luciana, with Vitor Luiz, also a principal dancer at San Francisco Ballet. In 2013 she acted in another film, *American Mongrel*, and returned to performing with San Francisco Ballet.

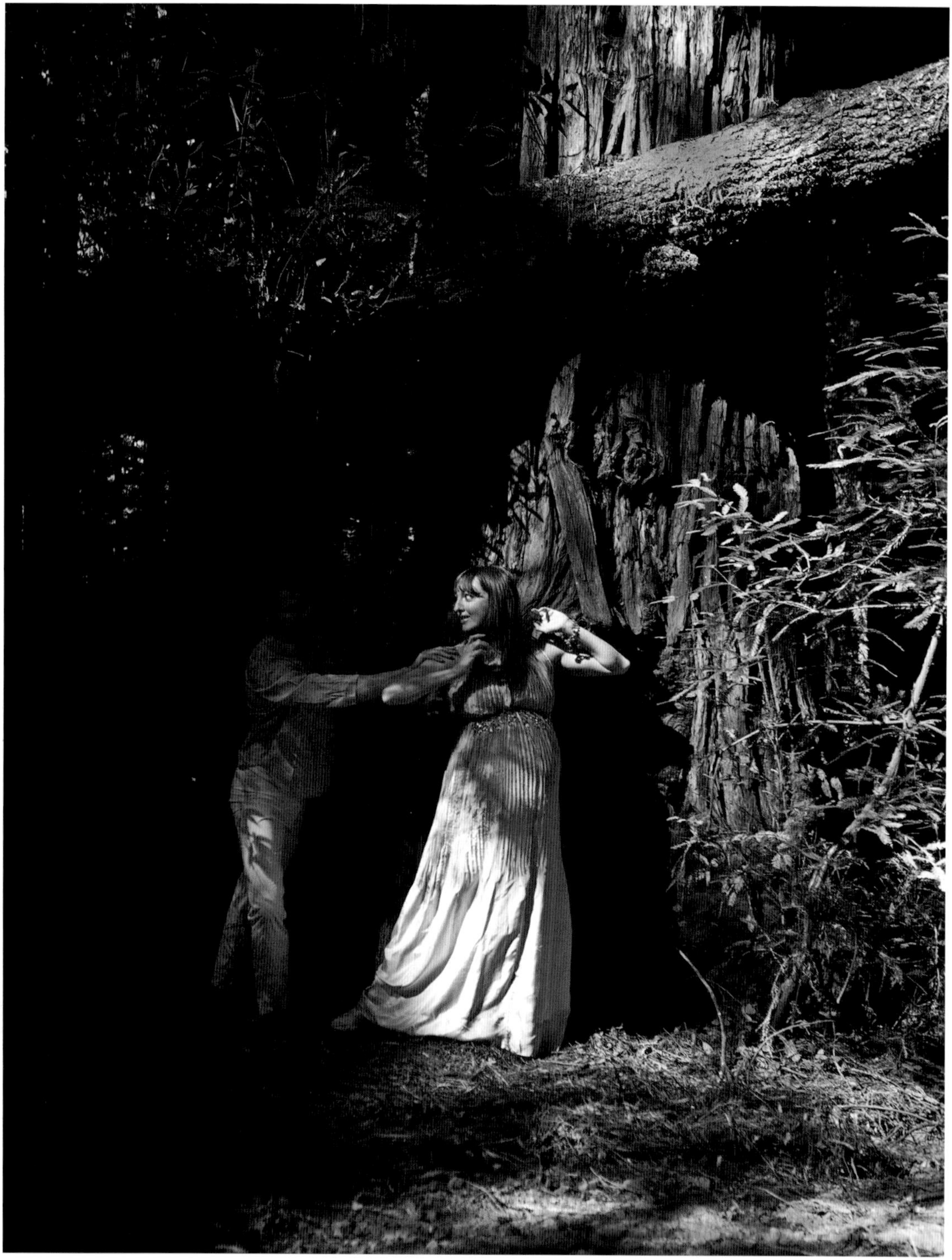

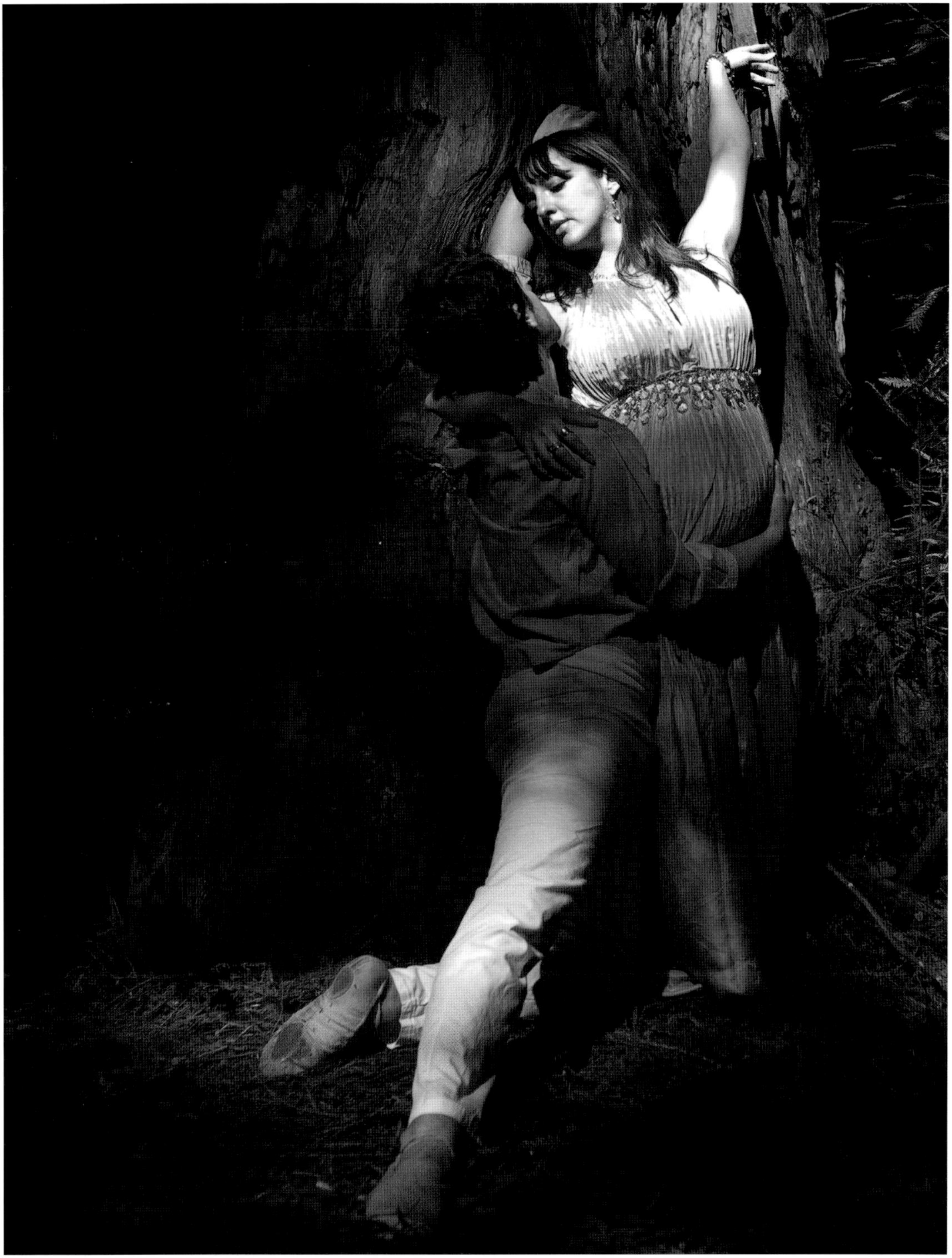

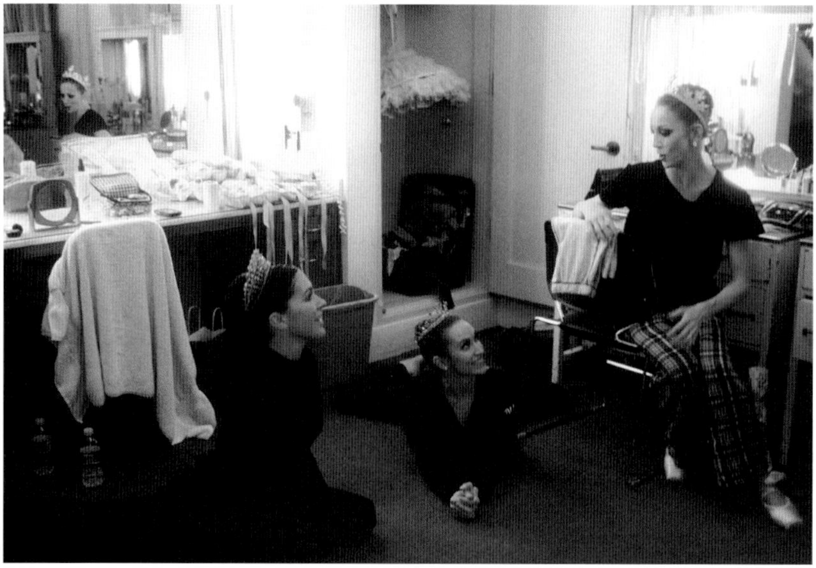

The dressing room the three princesses shared from 1999 to 2009, during the making of this book. (2008)

All three dancers continued to receive glowing praise after having children:

KRISTIN LONG

"Ravishing…airy, fast and truly unforgettable."

– SAN FRANCISCO *CHRONICLE*, APRIL 2002

"Evincing the qualities one most wishes to see in a dancer: instinct and expressiveness."

– LONDON *TIMES LITERARY SUPPLEMENT*, SEPTEMBER 2001

"Kristin Long has never looked more in her element."

– *DANCE VIEW TIMES*, JANUARY 2007

TINA LeBLANC

"Continues to dazzle in the fire and precision of her dancing."

–SAN FRANCISCO *EXAMINER*, FEBRUARY 2002

"[LeBlanc, having] returned to the stage after a second maternity leave, is as luxuriantly musical, technically sparkling and generous-hearted as ever."

– SAN FRANCISCO *CHRONICLE*, DECEMBER 2003

"LeBlanc is the kind of dancer who makes me glad somebody invented ballet."

– *BALLETTALK*, DECEMBER 2008

KATITA WALDO

"I have never seen Waldo look so genuinely radiant and move with such natural ease."

–LONDON *EVENING STANDARD*, SEPTEMBER 2001

"An artist in total command of her medium."

–*BALLET.MAGAZINE*, JANUARY 2006

"Such inventive dance, surgically delivered, is a rare delight."

– SAN JOSE *MERCURY NEWS*, MAY 2013

I am grateful beyond measure to Katita Waldo, Kristin Long, and Tina LeBlanc for their unceasing dedication to this project. I thank their respective husbands, Marshall Crutcher, Michael Locicero and Martin West, and Marco Jerkunica, for their astounding kindness and generosity. And to their children, James; Kai, Hannah, and Jonah; and Marinko and Sasha: I hope you see in these pictures a glimpse of the bliss you have brought into this world.

Supreme thanks to my husband, David Thomson; to Alexandria Albers and Sara Bader for understanding what this book is about and what contribution it might make; to my stepdaughter Rachel, for giving the title that stuck; to my son Zachary, who ably assisted me on shoots throughout his childhood; to Mark Morris, who contributed an early piece of writing for the book and gave me the great pleasure of photographing him while he created a dance; and to the brilliant and dear Hilton Als, who gives to theater in all of its guises; to Sara Stemen, Mia Johnson, Janet Behning, Andrea Chlad, and Diane Levinson at Princeton Architectural Press, for artfully shaping the book into what it has become; and to Troy Peters and Griff Williams at Gallery 16 for so much careful and expert work with the images; at the San Francisco Ballet: the dancers, especially Lorena Feijoo and Vitor Luiz, and the technical staff; Helgi Tomasson; Glenn McCoy; Ashley Wheater; Linda Twitchell; Diane Kounalakis; and Kyra Jablonsky; at San Francisco Public Library: Katherine Bella and Everett Erlandson; at Stanford University: Diane Middlebrook, Tobias Wolff, Fred Stout, Victoria Stewart, and Londa Schiebinger; at Art Museum of the Americas: Fabian Goncalves Borrega and to Shayla Dopp for Kai and his tutu made of sparklers. For their support of many stripes on this project, I am indebted to friends Leah Garchik, Katherine Berkeley, Susan Rugtiv, Susan Levine, Stacey Case, Sunnie Evers, Holly Goldberg Sloan and Gary Rosen, Anne Herlihy and Ben Woolverton, Jamie and Philip Bowles, Virginia and Alan Jones, and David and Pam Packard; to my cousin Rachel French Weber; to my siblings and their spouses: Juliet and Will Ganschow, Joe Sherer and Caroline Mead, Paul and Jennifer Sherer, Brian and Katrina Sherer; and to our tireless, persevering mother, Juliette Reilly.